SOCRATIC CIRCLES

SOCRATIC

Fostering Critical and Creative Thinking

CIRCLES

in Middle and High School

MATT COPELAND

Stenhouse Publishers
Portland, Maine

Stenhouse Publishers
www.stenhouse.com

Copyright © 2005 by Matt Copeland

Library of Congress Cataloging-in-Publication Data
Copeland, Matt, 1975–
     Socratic circles : fostering critical and creative thinking in middle and
high school / Matt Copeland.
     p. cm.
     Includes bibliographical references.
     ISBN 1-57110-394-5 (alk. paper)
     1. Questioning. 2. Critical thinking. 3. Creative thinking. 4. Middle
school teaching. 5. High school teaching. I. Title.
LB1027.44.C66 2005
373.1102—dc22   2004062647

Cover and interior design by Martha Drury
Cover photograph by Matt Copeland

Manufactured in the United States of America on acid-free paper
12 11 10 09 08   12 11 10 9 8 7 6 5

For my students—

Thanks for all the lessons you've taught me

Contents

Chapter 8
ASSESSMENT AND FOLLOW–UP ACTIVITIES

Introduction

On the first day of school, James entered my classroom several minutes before the tardy bell, making sure no one else was in the room. He slammed his books on a desk and said firmly, "Just so you know, I hate English and there is absolutely nothing you can do to change that."

Standing at five feet six inches, James had a smile and a charm that usually helped him talk his way through any situation. He was a bright and verbose young man with a great deal of bravado and swagger that carried over from the fields of athletic competition. His successes on the soccer field ensured his popularity, and his sense of humor and smile made him shine. In class, however, James lacked focus and direction. The qualities that made him a celebrity among his peers also made him resented and, at times, despised. His passion and energy often led him into trouble with his teachers and peers alike. His exuberance and strong will turned off many fellow students to his ideas, not because of what he said but because of how he said it.

As tempting as it was to fire back with a sarcastic comment after James's outburst on the first day of class, I bit my tongue and masked my pain with a smile of my own. That was the last time I heard James say that he hated English, but I've never forgotten those words. In fact, as I look back on them now, I realize just how crucial and revealing they were. James needed to vent; he needed to blow off some steam. His frustration was not directed at me. It was not even directed at the content of my class. James was unhappy with himself and his abilities. He dreamed of gaining more from English class and more from himself. When I met James as a high school junior, he was one credit behind his peers in English, labeled an "at-risk" student in jeopardy of not graduating on time, and abhorred English class.

By the end of his senior year, James's dream was coming true. He was concurrently enrolled in three English classes (by choice), was going to graduate on time, and had decided that English was going to be his college major. Now a Division I soccer player at a university in the Midwest, James has continued his growth and found many of the answers and resolutions he was looking for. If you ask James what was responsible for such a dramatic transformation in his life, his answer will be encased in that same soccer-field smile and swagger; his answer will be Socratic circles.

I had the privilege of working with James during the two-year period when I first began implementing Socratic circles in my classroom. As a first-year teacher, I was frustrated with my students' poor reading abilities and habits. I was frustrated with their lack of critical thought and creativity. I was frustrated with their complete unwillingness to engage in discussion. During my first year of teaching, my students clearly communicated to me their belief in the philosophy that education is a passive activity. I struggled all year long to help them overcome that belief, but to no avail.

That summer I searched high and low for something—anything—that might help alleviate my students' apathy. I wanted a strategy that asked them to probe below the surface meaning of what they read, one that allowed them to think creatively and critically, one that stimulated discussion in my classroom that made learning active and engaging, rather than an exercise in passivity. In scouring the research and other pedagogical publications and in talking with peers and colleagues, sifting through strategy after strategy, one idea kept reappearing: the Socratic seminar.

After that discovery, and in the five years since as I have modified and adapted this practice to fit my classroom and my students, I have begun to achieve my dream of turning students into critical consumers of all forms of literacy. Socratic seminars can be structured and can appear very different from one classroom to the next. In fact, even the names applied to the strategy can vary greatly: a "Socratic seminar" here, a "fishbowl conversation" there, an "open forum" across the way. In talking with colleagues and adapting my use of this strategy, I've settled on the practice outlined in this book, *Socratic Circles*.

Socratic circles are the best activity that takes place in my classroom, bar none, and I am convinced that their power will unlock doors for both fellow teachers and their students. The results that manifest themselves in front of a teacher's eyes are mesmerizing. For teachers who seek to instill learning skills in their students that will carry them through life long after they have left the confines of the classroom, Socratic circles offer a portion of the answer.

Socratic circles turn partial classroom control, classroom direction, and classroom governance over to students by creating a truly equitable learning community where the weight and value of student voices and teacher voices are indistinguishable from each other. What might appear to be random chaos to the naked eye of a hallway passerby is, in fact, the careful implementation of a method of philosophy more than 2,400 years old.

Socratic circles change the way individuals read, think, discuss, write, and act; they have the power to change a student's perspective on living, learning, and behaving. Critical reading, critical thinking, discussion skills, listening skills, team-building skills, vocabulary improvement, and student ownership, voice, and empowerment are all valid reasons for including Socratic circles in the classroom. But perhaps more important is the reality that Socratic circles foster in students a new way of looking at the world around them. One of the keys to creating lifelong learners—students who continue the quest for knowledge and understanding long after they have exited our classrooms—is contained within the magic of Socratic circles.

In a time when our students are being inundated with increasing numbers of standardized tests and an increased push to have the "correct" answers at all times, they have less and less time to work on the critical and creative thinking skills that will ultimately facilitate their growth and development into productive, responsible citizens. Socratic circles are one strategy that provides this opportunity while still having students practice and polish skills in a wide variety of other curricular areas, including reading, speaking, listening, and vocabulary.

Our students need practice and instruction in working collaboratively to solve problems, making decisions, and determining meaning. The activity in our classrooms should not always concern itself with students knowing the right answers; sometimes it should concern itself with students asking the right questions. With the help of Socratic circles and effective circle leaders, our students can be empowered to do just that.

This book is designed to help teachers begin using Socratic circles in their own practice. This strategy can be adapted in numerous ways and modified to fit a wide range of classrooms from the elementary to the college level. It is my hope that the book provides the necessary background and framework to help teachers start thinking, designing, and constructing an arrangement for the use of Socratic circles in their own teaching and that it can be a continuing resource for them as their own practice and experience begin to grow.

The first chapter outlines the reasons and purposes for implementing Socratic circles into the classroom routine. Chapters 2, 3, 4, and 5 explain in detail the process and procedures of Socratic circles and offer insight and helpful hints into making them work. Chapter 6, then, shows an example Socratic circle from my own classroom to reveal how students perform in these situations and how these skills blend together to create a cohesive whole. Extension activities, follow-up activities, and methods of assessment are outlined in Chapters 7 and 8 to help align the strategy with the curriculum and help students make connections between their discussions and other content material.

At the beginning of each chapter, I have also included student dialogue inspired by some of the critical reading and thinking we have done in my classroom. Rather than transcribing this dialogue directly, I have chosen to remove many of the "likes," "umms," "you knows," and other snippets of teenage vernacular, not only for the purposes of readability but also to help the reader focus on the collaborative thinking in which the students are engaged. Through these examples, and the interactions and insight within each, I hope readers begin to see the growth and learning Socratic circles can facilitate.

In many ways, this book is a celebration of the power and influence of dialogue. If it weren't for the ongoing assistance of my colleagues, through their thoughts, ideas, questions, reassurances, and beratings, these pages in front of you might never have been written. Their help has been indispensable. Among them are Bryan Anderson, Lawrence Baines, Jerrod Bohn, John Bushman, Annette Collins, John Franklin, Jeff Handley, Judy Hayn, Annie Heidersbach, Chris Goering, Todd Goodson, Marc Grout, Dara Oswald, Sam Rockford, Julie Samuels, Ingrid Seitz, and Bill Varner. Thanks.

Socratic circles have changed the way I teach. They have made my classroom a more open, inviting place, where students want to be and want to learn. They have transformed my practice and philosophy and have created a community that fosters active, engaged learning. I once dreamed of a classroom where true learning was a noble endeavor that stimulated the minds, hearts, and imaginations of students, a classroom that instilled a desire to explore life and the world beyond its walls. With the help of the classroom dialogue created through Socratic circles, I've realized that dream.

Chapter 1

THE BENEFITS OF SOCRATIC CIRCLES

BRITTANY: *Obviously she's upset that Arizona got rid of poetry in all of their classes.*

JIMMY: *What makes you say that?*

BRITTANY: *Look at the lines and the way she worded things, even in the first stanza—"interdicted . . . evicted . . . squanders." It's like she's just screaming at the governor.*

STEPHANIE: *I agree. She thinks this is a total mistake, and she's trying to convince others she's right so that maybe people will realize their mistake before it's too late.*

TYLER: *Too late for what?*

STEPHANIE: *Too late for poetry. If people grew up without learning about poetry, none of us would understand it. It's like a whole art form would be lost forever.*

JIMMY: *It's not like poetry is difficult. I'm sure people could still figure it out even if it wasn't taught in school. I don't understand what she's so mad about.*

JOSE: *You're probably right. People probably would still be able to figure out poetry, but I'm not sure they would figure it out as well or if it would mean as much if we didn't learn about it in school. I mean, every time I read a new poem, it gets easier, and what I learn in one poem I can usually use in another poem.*

STEPHANIE: *You lost me.*

JOSE: *Okay. Like right here in the middle of the poem she says, "where the fans overhead / whispered 'I am, I am' in iambic pentameter." If it wasn't for studying poetry in school, I'd have no idea what iambic pentameter was. And I certainly wouldn't pick up on the idea that the noise the fan blades make sounds like iambic pentameter.*

BRITTANY: *Yeah, that makes sense. The more you learn about something, the more you are going to understand it.*

JOSE: *I think it's more than that, though. I think that's her whole point.*

STEPHANIE: *What's her whole point?*

JOSE: *She's saying that if poetry isn't taught in school, if we don't learn about all the tricks and devices poets use, then we won't be able to understand her, we won't understand all the poetry that's going on around us all the time.*

BRITTANY: *I get it. We become like poetry morons who don't understand or appreciate the beauty of poetry, whether it's written poetry or natural poetry, like the storm and the rain in the last stanza. Then she has no one to communicate with, no one to share what she writes with, and we all just sit there dumb. That's what she's angry about.*

JOSE: *Exactly.*

In November 1999, after three long months working and struggling each week to better understand the material of the class and one another, students enrolled in my freshman English class finally got it. A collection of once downcast, uninspired expressions suddenly lighted up with wisdom, understanding, and purpose. Seated in the center of my room in two concentric circles, students appeared to freeze in their places, savoring and enjoying the moment, only their eyes moving as if in a slow waltz from face to face. And at each stop around the circle, as their eyes slowly traveled from peer to peer, something deep within them was surging to the surface, ready to erupt. Only after the first face cracked at the corners of the mouth and the smiles of self-satisfaction, accomplishment, and success became contagious throughout the room, did those student eyes fall to me, their teacher. And at that moment, after three months of my own frustration and soul-searching, I knew something magical had just happened for my students.

The conversation above represents a "lightbulb" moment when suddenly the class curriculum, real-world life skills, and the discovery of personal meaning and relevance all erupted within our classroom. Suddenly what we studied and learned in the classroom, even the intricacies of poetry and iambic pentameter, seemed urgent and important. The result was a group of students with a deep understanding of a selection of text, improved skills in comprehension, vocabulary, listening, speaking, and critical thinking, and experience in working together to construct meaning, solve problems, and explore life connections. The method for helping students to achieve this learning was the strategy known as Socratic circles.

A BRIEF HISTORY

More than 2,400 years ago, Socrates believed there was a more effective and productive way of teaching students than the lecture. He believed that within each of his students resided an often-untapped reservoir of knowledge and understanding. And by helping students examine their premonitions and beliefs while at the same time accepting the limitations of human thought, Socrates believed students could improve their reasoning skills and ultimately move toward more rational thinking and ideas more easily supported with logic. The methodology he used to accomplish this has come to be known as Socratic questioning.

Modern education appears obsessed with answers—both correct and incorrect. It is questions, however, that drive the human mind in critical thought. Elder and Paul (1998) note, "Questions define tasks, express problems, and delineate issues. Answers, on the other hand, often signal a full stop in thought. Only when an answer generates a further question does thought continue its life as such" (p. 297). Typically, teachers ask questions because we hope the answers will represent a final destination of learning and thought, a kind of educational checklist where either "yes," this learning has occurred, or "no," this learning has not occurred. We must push our students through this initial barrier of surface meaning, show them that all thinking involves the asking of questions, and reveal that the asking of one question leads to the asking of further questions. It is the ongoing, honest quest for information and understanding through the act of questioning that embodies the true ideal of democratic education.

Socratic questioning, then, greatly assists us in this endeavor. The purpose here is to use questioning to bring forward already held ideas in the students' minds, to make them more aware and cognizant of the learning and understanding that has already occurred. Adler (1984) defines this concept as "questioning students about something they have read so as to help them improve their understanding of basic ideas and values" (pp. 17–18). With this goal in sight, the idea of Socratic questioning is incredibly valuable in reviving student minds made numb to critical thought.

Socratic questioning is a systematic process for examining the ideas, questions, and answers that form the basis of human belief. It involves recognizing that all new understanding is linked to prior understanding, that thought itself is a continuous thread woven through our lives rather than isolated sets of questions and answers. As teachers, we must help students recognize that all thoughts are based on prior thoughts and that current thoughts will build a foundation for future thoughts. We must help students see that all thinking is flawed and incomplete, that all ideas can be further developed and better explained, and that questioning helps us explore these realities. It is by following every statement with a question to further explore the depth of our thinking that we allow our ideas to grow and develop more deeply. In the classroom, this concept is incredibly important, especially in breaking the habits of students preprogrammed to think that all questions have one, and only one, correct answer.

In 1982 Mortimer Adler published *The Paideia Proposal: An Educational Manifesto* in which he described an extension of the current and most predominant mode of instruction. Adler outlined "a mode of teaching called 'maieutic' because it helps the student bring ideas to birth" (p. 29). He suggested that it is not enough to simply lecture to our students and hope they acquire the skills that educators deem necessary for them to have. We must teach "by asking questions, by leading discussions, by helping students to raise their minds up from a state of understanding or appreciating less to a state of understanding or appreciating more" (Adler 1982, p. 29). Adler went on to propose that the method to achieve this goal was to engage students' minds "in the study of individual works of merit, whether they be literary or otherwise, accompanied by a discussion of the ideas, the values, and the forms embodied in such products of human art" (p. 29).

Adler himself derived this idea from the annals of history, his own experience, and the experiences of colleagues in the world of education. The Great Books movement, originally developed between 1910 and 1940 by Alexander Meiklejohn at Amherst College, John Erskine at Columbia University, Stringfellow Barr and Scott Buchanan at the University of Virginia, and Adler and Robert Hutchins at the University of Chicago, began incorporating Socratic inquiry into their curriculum and developed the framework for the current pedagogical practice. The term "Socratic seminar" appears to have first been coined by Scott Buchanan in his work with the St. John's College New Program (Strong 1996, p. 5), and the idea has continued with organizations such as The Center for Socratic Practice, The Touchstones Project, Junior Great Books, the National Paideia Center, and the Coalition of Essential Schools. Over time, the strategy has grown and been adapted as various educators—Dennis Gray, Lesley Lambright, and Margaret Metzger, among others—began applying it to their own classrooms, curricular content, and the learning of their own students. The version of Socratic circles described in this book is no different; it is a modification and an extension of the principles and methodology of Socratic seminars started in the 1920s.

UNDERSTANDING SOCRATIC CIRCLES

One of Adler's admirers, Lesley Lambright (1995), defines a Socratic seminar as an "exploratory intellectual conversation centered on a text" (p. 30). However, it is the nature and process of that conversation that differs radically from the typical teacher-led, question-and-answer discussion. A Socratic circle turns the vast majority of the guidance of the conversation and the ownership of the material over to the students. Because of this ownership students are more motivated and involved in the learning that takes place within the classroom, and in my own classes, students report that these Socratic circles create learning that they think is more meaningful and applicable to their lives and futures.

At first some students are apprehensive about this type of self-governance and control in the classroom; often their education experience has been with teachers firmly in control. What alleviates this trepidation in the students' minds is the structure and organization of the strategy itself. Students learn quickly that the process and ground rules of Socratic circles provide the framework for the conversation they will engage in and that they themselves will police the progress made.

Typically, Socratic circles are built upon a foundation of the following components: a short passage of text that students have read critically, and two concentric circles of students, one circle focusing on exploring the meaning expressed in the text and a second circle observing the conversation. After the first circle has examined and discussed the text, the second circle provides feedback on the quality of the dialogue that took place and the individual and group dynamics that facilitated that dialogue. After this period of reflection, the two circles of students change places and roles, and the process repeats itself with new voices and new ideas in each circle. Of course there are many variations to each aspect of Socratic circles, but maintaining the discussion-feedback-reverse pattern is essential. It is the interaction between the inner and outer circles that enables students to control the direction and process of the dialogue taking place.

Where Socratic circles begin to differ from typical classroom discussion is in the fact that students are required to remain silent while filling certain roles. While the inner circle is discussing the text, the members of the outer circle are instructed to imagine they are scientific observers behind a two-way mirror; they are able to see and hear everything going on, but they cannot interact with the inner circle in any way. Likewise, while the outer circle is providing feedback about the quality of discussion that took place, the members of the inner circle must listen in silence.

Socratic circles offer a type of real-world, student-centered learning where the teacher acts only to keep the discussion moving forward, regardless of the discussion's direction. It is the students, not the teacher, who guide and direct the focus of the conversation. As students construct their discussion, they are activating prior knowledge, making connections, and synthesizing new schemata "in a collaborative quest for understanding . . . dedicated to achieving an enlarged understanding of a text, not merely ingesting it" (Gray 1992, pp. 17–18).

SOCRATIC CIRCLES AND LITERATURE CIRCLES

Socratic circles and literature circles share many of the same attributes. With each strategy, students are discussing a work that they have read and experienced and are combining their own ideas with the ideas of their peers to create new learning and understanding. And with both strategies, students assume the responsibility for organizing and discussing the textual material, no matter what format it takes. However, there are also key differences in the strategies. Literature circles typically involve a smaller number of students, and each student completes a specific role within the group to maximize the coverage of the conversation. On the other hand, Socratic circles involve larger groups of students without specific roles and seek to include a more diverse range of opinions and perspectives within the conversation. Perhaps the most obvious difference between literature circles and Socratic circles is the element of student choice in reading material. Whereas several literature circles covering multiple works may be going on in a classroom at any given time, Socratic circles focus the attention of all students within a class on one, typically teacher-selected, piece of text.

Despite these differences, the underlying constructivist philosophy upon which both strategies are built suggests that students are coming together to build meaning and understanding in a collaborative fashion with their peers. In fact, I prefer to intersperse these strategies in my classes and have found the practice to be both a rewarding experience for students and an effective method to enhance their skills within each strategy. Socratic circles offer more teacher guidance and coaching in the process of mutual inquiry and help students develop the habits of thought and analysis that lead to improved literature circles. Likewise, the smaller groups of literature circles help students develop their own voices and practice expressing and sharing their ideas with peers, improving their abilities and making them more comfortable in doing the same in the larger groups of Socratic circles. Many teachers use Socratic circles to teach students the skills needed for effective literature circles, but the strategies complement each other nicely and can enhance the literature instruction of any classroom.

In my classes students often engage in Socratic circles and literature circles simultaneously. Typically, students in my classes choose the novels or other longer works they are reading from a short list that centers on a particular theme or idea. This means that although students have choice in what they read and discuss with peers in their literature circles, we can also engage in whole-class discussion that traces the theme or ideas through each of the books. This is particularly effective when the selection of text for our Socratic circle explores this same theme or idea. Students can draw examples and illustrations from the work being read in their literature circle and share them with the class, helping other students understand and gain exposure to many different books. In this way, students maintain their voices and choices through literature circles and gain practice in applying the knowledge they are gaining to our Socratic circles.

DEVELOPING STUDENTS' ACADEMIC SKILLS

Socratic circles are an excellent means of developing a wide range of academic skills. Beyond capturing the imagination and creativity, Socratic circles can build skills in the areas of reading, listening, reflection, critical thinking, and participation. A benefit of Socratic circles is that they bring all the areas of the curriculum and instruction together into a cohesive whole. No longer must teachers teach a fragmented curriculum where by late October students have already forgotten what they learned in September. With Socratic circles, teachers can integrate their curriculum into a seamless package in which students continuously build and develop a variety of skills.

Critical Thinking

Perhaps what Socratic circles offer students and teachers more than anything is the opportunity to practice and hone their skills in critical thinking. In most classroom discussion, the teacher poses a question to a student and one of three things happens. The student either answers the question with the answer the teacher was hoping for, answers the question with an answer the teacher was not looking for, or simply responds with "I don't know." And typically the teacher responds in one of three ways: praise, disapproval, or encouraging the student to try again. In all three cases, the latent curriculum of this process teaches students that critical thinking is an ability that some students possess and some do not. Socratic questioning helps to correct this problem. If, after each student response to a question, the teacher follows up with another question that further explores the perspective of the answer, the agenda underlying the answer, or the application of concepts that produced the answer, students quickly see critical thought as an ongoing, developing skill rather than some secretive society to which some students belong and others do not.

Let me explain this idea in another way. In recent history we have changed the way we instruct students to write; we have moved from simply *assigning* writing to *teaching* writing, focusing on the process rather than just the product. We have our students brainstorm and engage in prewriting to generate ideas. We have them draft their ideas and then revise and edit to improve the quality of the expression of those ideas. We encourage our students to believe that good writing develops from hard work in drafting, revising, and redrafting, that good writing simply does not magically appear. Critical thinking is no different than writing. Both are processes that challenge us to revise and improve our ideas for the benefit of our own understanding and the understanding of others. And in both cases, it is the process of Socratic questioning that helps us revise and improve the quality of our ideas.

Critical thinking must be viewed as a process, just as we approach writing. We teach our students that no piece of writing is ever "finished," that there is always something that could be improved or expanded upon that would make our writing more complete, more substantial, more effective. Our thinking is no different. At the end of the day, our writing, our thinking, and our lives are merely "rough drafts," works in progress to which a new day will bring new experiences and new improvements; we must simply open ourselves to the possibilities. We help our students practice the writing process almost daily, but rarely do we devote as much time or attention to teaching the process of critical thinking. As Elder and Paul (1998) suggest, "The goal of critical thinking is to establish a disciplined 'executive' level of thinking, a powerful inner voice of reason, to monitor, assess, and reconstitute—in a more rational direction—our thinking, feeling, and action" (p. 300). Socratic questioning and Socratic circles are ways teachers can encourage students to view critical thinking as a lifelong, life-actualizing process.

In my classes, students begin to see this type of thinking evolve within their own minds through our participation in Socratic circles. One student, Pablo, reveals how he applies this type of thinking to his life outside the classroom:

I have learned how to think in an entirely new way. Now, whenever I am doing something, or perhaps even watching TV, I think about why certain phrases are significant and why the writer uses them. I even think if they might symbolize something else. I do not dislike this new form of thinking; in fact it is helpful.

Clyde reflects on his growth in critical thinking because of Socratic circles and compares it with the learning he does in most of his other classes. His reflections reveal his emerging understanding that critical thinking and learning itself are ongoing processes rather than collections of learning products.

> *Sometimes I feel like education is more about facts and memorizing than anything else. However, is that really learning? I think developing your skills of absorbing, processing, and expressing those ideas and facts is more important and more beneficial. I enjoy learning facts and concepts, but what is even more enjoyable is the theories and ideas I can discuss, think and reason about with others.*

At the heart of Clyde's comments is the idea that through more engaged dialogue with classmates centered on the concepts and knowledge his class is exploring, learning becomes a more valuable endeavor that taps student interest and enjoyment.

Creativity

Creativity is another area greatly improved through Socratic circles. Lambright (1995) points out that students "are more creative when they are engaged in a group, listening to the thinking of others, watching the play of one idea bouncing off another, while being encouraged to dig below the surface of thought and feeling. Transactions spark the imagination" (p. 33). The active nature and the creativity of the analysis and support of arguments within a Socratic circle encourage students to be creative themselves. It is the "interrogative or discussion method of [Socratic circles that] stimulate the imagination and intellect by awakening the creative and inquisitive powers. In no other way can children's understanding of what they know be improved" (Adler 1982, p. 29). The stimulation of all the various types of thinking and learning allows students to grow and develop into complete, holistic individuals. Carol explains,

> *I have to admit that when we first started Socratic circles I thought to myself, "What in the world am I supposed to get out of this?" I didn't see the point, and honestly I didn't believe in them. I just thought it was something we did so you didn't have to teach. Slowly, though, I began to realize how often I thought about Socratic circles outside of class and how often I was inspired to write about what we discussed. Not essays, but just write. And when I look back now, I see how they've helped me grow as a person, how they've made me someone I'm proud of.*

Because their creativity is stimulated, students are able to find mediums to express themselves and unique ways to display the products of their own ideas and thinking. In my own practice, I have witnessed this phenomenon on several occasions. I am always amazed at how the dialogue within a Socratic circle moves students to engage in further study and thought on their own. Many times students return to class the day after their dialogue to share some further idea they have discovered, whether by their own thought or by research. Some students even go so far as to produce some body of work inspired by our discussion. Whether a piece of writing, a piece of artwork, interpretive dance, music, or some other means, students find ways to filter their critical thinking through their own creative channels and produce new work that reveals the connections to the central ideas and material we have been studying.

Critical Reading

Metzger (1998) suggests "[a]s citizens, parents, and reading adults, we worry about our children's inadequate reading skills. Although many students can decode, most are superficial readers, comprehending only surface information" (p. 240). Incorporating reading strategies and activities into our classrooms that move students beyond basic reading comprehension and into higher-order thinking is critical to our curricula. Arnold, Hart, and Campbell (1988) observed that after they implemented Socratic circles in their classrooms, their students were "gaining deeper understanding of literature and heightened interest in reading and writing. They are learning to think critically and to respect the opinions of their peers" (p. 48).

In my own classes I have witnessed students who never expressed much interest in or placed value on interpreting literature suddenly finding meaning and relevance in the process. Several of my students who described themselves as "noncollege bound" found that, for the first time in their schooling careers, interpreting literature and other text was something that was not handed down to them from experts, but a living, breathing process that was created spontaneously through intellectual discourse. Mandy comments on this reality and explains how the idea of reading has changed for both her and her peers.

> *In Socratic circles you have to think in a different way. You can't just read the text and automatically see a deeper meaning. You have to think about what it could mean and relate the text to other works or experiences you are familiar with, which isn't a skill we use often.*

I have witnessed my students applying to standardized testing some of these same skills of critical reading, developed in the course of Socratic circles. When handed a passage to read and questions to answer at the end, many of my students use many of the same techniques we use to analyze a Socratic circle selection of text from a critical reading perspective: they identify new vocabulary words, underline key phrases, note repetition of words, phrases, and structure, and jot down questions that help them to better explore meaning. Robert, another student who self-identifies as "noncollege bound," echoes Mandy's comments and explains how his reading and learning have improved.

> *Socratic circles have given me the ability to look farther into a text I am reading, and I can comprehend better with what I read also. I feel I can learn much easier because I take more things into consideration.*

Developing a Lifelong Love of Reading

Equally important as developing skills in reading critically is developing an interest and a passion for the activity of reading itself, ideally, developing students into lifelong readers and learners. Davey, a student with special needs in my classroom who suffers from problems with concentration and attention, writes,

> *After our Socratic Circles, I have found myself reading more than I ever have before. I've actually started reading every day, which is odd because I rarely ever read before and I didn't care to. Socratic circles have made me want to better myself.*

The poor reading skills of our nation's youth is a disturbing reality. Socratic circles enable students to work collaboratively to improve their reading skills. Through the repeated readings and the thorough analysis of the material, students learn to take their time while reading and explore possible multiple meanings and interpretations.

Speaking

As teachers of the language arts, we all encourage our students to participate in class discussions. Some of us even assign a portion of the student's overall grade to participation. We find ways to motivate student contributions through praise and the affirmation of ideas, and at times, we require student comments by progressing down class rosters or drawing names from a hat. Regardless, there are always some students who contribute and participate in class discussions at a minimal level, some only when required to, and some not even then. Although Socratic circles cannot change this reality, they can improve it.

Because of the collaborative nature of these conversations, students learn that all contributions, even the ones that appear tangential or erroneous on the surface, can help the group develop their ideas and move toward their discovery of meaning. Students then are held accountable to their peers, rather than the teacher, for sharing ideas and contributing to the group. When faced with this reality, many students develop a stronger voice in the classroom and are more willing to participate. Carol was one such student. At the beginning of the school year, she was a quiet, shy young woman who spoke in class only when asked or when spoken to, and she was equally quiet in the hallways and lunchroom with her peers.

> *I've learned through Socratic circles that I can't be timid about saying my thoughts and feelings. I think early on I hurt my groups by not saying anything because maybe my ideas could have been the spark that aided in finding meaning. By the end, though, I started sharing my ideas, and that allowed more of us to get into the discussion.*

Many students also report that developing these skills changes the way they view school and their own learning. Once initial skills in speaking are developed, students are able to expand into persuasive speaking and supporting their ideas with textual evidence. John, a student with aspirations of becoming a trial lawyer, shares his appreciation for the growth he has seen in his persuasive speaking abilities.

> *By having these Socratic circles I have learned to say what I feel and use evidence to defend my position. Before I would just say what I thought and let it dangle, like raw meat in front of a pack of wild dogs. People would tear my thoughts to shreds because in my mind I had nothing to back those ideas up. Now I am able to assertively state what I think and prove to anyone that my ideas can be applied to the subject and learned from.*

Socratic circles encourage students to pull themselves from the silence of the classroom's shadows and become more active and vocal learning participants. They not only allow students to become more comfortable with speaking in classroom discussions, but help them develop skills in speaking persuasively and supporting their ideas with references to textual evidence.

Listening

As Adler (1983) says, "Listening, like reading, is primarily an activity of the mind, not of the ear or the eye. When the mind is not actively involved in the process, it should be called hearing, not listening; seeing, not reading" (pp. 85–86). The structure of Socratic circles is such that students learn quickly to improve their learning so that what they hear with their ears allows them to listen with their minds. During the feedback sessions, students are quick to point out when students are not listening to one another. They see and understand how detrimental poor listening skills can be to the quality of discussion and act quickly to encourage a solution to the problem.

Kent comments on this truth and reveals how high-quality listening can greatly influence the quality of dialogue and learning in the classroom.

> *In Socratic circles you learn to be patient and to listen to the thoughts, feelings, and ideas of others when you're both on the outside and inside circle. Through listening, you hear multiple theories and opinions over the meaning of certain lines and the overall meaning the author is trying to convey. By listening, your thoughts and opinions might change, depending on what reasons others give for a certain topic.*

It is through listening that students are encouraged to contemplate differing opinions and points of view that sometimes challenge their own deeply held beliefs. Once students learn to open their minds to the views of others, they begin to realize that their own ideas can be expanded. It is not that their opinions are being replaced with the opinions of others, but by accepting that other points of view are possible, students begin to form a context of opinion in which their individual views fit. This serves students in both an academic and social sense. Sally, who began my class as a rather obstinate and opinionated student, reflects on her personal and social growth in the area of listening.

> *Before we started Socratic circles, I was probably the most stubborn person to talk to. I was not a good listener. Because of being "forced" to understand others' viewpoints, I have greatly improved that part of my character.*

To become active discussion participants, students must first learn to listen to one another's ideas. Without being able to listen carefully and attentively, they will never gain the social skills necessary to become effective members of a democratic discussion.

Writing Skills

In my classes, students who have engaged in Socratic circles are able to think more expansively about the philosophical underpinnings of their selected topics and are able to produce writing that is more insightful, relevant, and thought-provoking than their peers who have not benefited from exposure to Socratic circles. Michaela reflects on how dialogue with her classmates allows her to use higher-order thinking skills and helps her expand her ideas.

> *Having a chance to take a piece of text, analyze it in my own way, and then discuss this text with a group hits on all of the critical skills needed to write analytical essays. Without Socratic circles, it would be very difficult for me to write an essay of any quality.*

Daniel echoes these same ideas and describes the dialogue created in Socratic circles as a valuable brainstorming or prewriting strategy that helps him explore his topic and structure his ideas.

> *Socratic circles help me to expand upon my ideas and pinpoint specifically what I want to say. They help me to organize my ideas in a more thoughtful way.*

In addition to developing the content of their writing, students also report that their participation in Socratic circles helps them examine more closely the craft of writing and explore specific techniques authors use to convey meaning. Because students are discussing these techniques with peers and with little or no influence from the teacher, they appear more willing to take chances on implementing those techniques in their writing. I've witnessed students in their own writing patterning specific sentence structure, grammar, punctuation, extended metaphors, parallelism, and other elements after selections of text they have discussed in Socratic circles much more willingly than when we discuss the same strategies as a whole class.

Beyond being more confident with their ideas and with incorporating new techniques into their writing, students are also much more comfortable with writing as a process and a learning endeavor and with their own abilities as writers. Because my students are allowed to generate ideas with peers in a collaborative dialogue, they think that the ideas they generate are more relevant, meaningful, and uniquely their own.

Critical Reflection

As students are building on reading, writing, discussion, and critical thinking skills, they are also growing in other important areas vital to future success. One of these areas is the capacity for reflective thinking. Reflective thinking involves mulling over past experiences, assessing one's own performance, and establishing goals for future performance. Socratic circles teach students to evaluate the quality of discussion not only in others but also in themselves. It is the critical reflection skills encouraged through feedback sessions that allow students to make comparisons and establish goals for their own discussions. Susan writes,

> *By looking back over our Socratic circles and listening to others, we received constructive criticism that helps us discuss and understand at a higher level. By taking time to reflect, we gain more, giving ourselves a chance to do better in the future.*

Likewise, reflective thinking allows students to become more aware of the processes of their own growth and learning; students are more cognizant of the workings of their own minds and are able to advocate for their own learning needs. Reflective thinking also helps draw all these various skills and curricula into a cohesive, unified whole linking learning to personal experience and to each student's future.

Adler (1982) suggests that Socratic circles teach "participants how to analyze their own minds as well as the thought of others, which is to say it engages students in disciplined conversation about ideas and values" (p. 30). This reflective thinking helps to improve student performance not only in Socratic circles, but in other academic areas as well. Through the experience of reflecting, assessing, and establishing goals, students develop confidence in both their abilities and their learning.

DEVELOPING STUDENTS' SOCIAL SKILLS

Not only are Socratic circles an ideal method to draw in various areas of the curricula and meet a wide variety of academic needs, but they also help build social skills that students will find useful in making personal and career decisions for the rest of their lives.

Team-Building Skills

As our society becomes more and more technologically advanced and our jobs move closer and closer to dealing with ideas and people and farther from dealing with raw materials, we are finding ourselves tackling work-related problems as members of teams rather than as individuals. However, the majority of people enter the workforce with very little knowledge and very little experience working as an equal member of a team. As Lambright (1995) says, Socratic circles "are team building situations. Through mutual inquiry in a cooperative setting, leaders and learners alike apply knowledge, making reasoned connections within themselves, with other group members, and with the text" (p. 34). In this way, students learn to voice their opinions and ideas in a positive, respectful, and cooperative manner. And because all participants (students and discussion leaders alike) come into the Socratic circle with a wide range of personal knowledge about the text, each participant becomes an equal partner in the group's quest for understanding. As Bruce writes,

> *As we began to discuss our ideas in Socratic circle after Socratic circle, I realized that sharing my own thoughts was not about the personal pursuit of glory, but about working with others to find one epiphany after another.*

It is this equity in personal experience that enables each participant to be viewed as a potential contributor. There are no preconceived roles, no preconceived assumptions about who will uncover the truth for the group. Students therefore come to each Socratic circle with a fresh start. They are able to practice working collaboratively on a problem from a common starting point.

Conflict Resolution

Another social skill that continues to be increasingly important in today's rapidly changing world is conflict resolution. Our students face a great deal of interpersonal challenges both in- and outside of school. Through Socratic circles, students have the opportunity to practice these skills in a controlled environment. Tredway (1995) points out that a Socratic circle "is an important occasion for students to confront such conflicts and actively work out solutions" (p. 28). As Jerry, a freshman, echoes,

> *Socratic circles taught us how to solve problems, to improve our writing and our critical thinking skills. But more than anything, they taught us how to deal with people and how to handle times when not everyone agreed.*

The process of Socratic circles helps build respect and understanding for students and their ideas and teaches participants to listen and accept multiple points of view. "This process by no means guarantees instantaneous respect for others, nor does it eliminate the conflict that is all too common in schools these days. It does, however, guide students to develop respectful, tactful, and kinder attitudes and behaviors" (Tredway 1995, p. 27). In fact, the benefits of Socratic circles in a middle school in Tennessee appear to have spread beyond the circles themselves: "[T]he

conflict resolution expertise demonstrated by [participants] was significantly higher than would normally be expected from a middle school
population" (Polite and Adams 1997, p. 265). However, simple conflict
resolution is only the tip of the iceberg. Students preferring noncon-
frontational resolutions to their disagreements is wonderful, but what is
also needed is tolerance and acceptance of multiple views. Polite and
Adams (1997) continue to explain that in their research "approximately
25% of all the students interviewed reported working to achieve win-win
outcomes" (p. 265).

Jessica, a student with an impressive ability to offer deep insight in
compact units of language, suggests, "Socratic circles are not only a way
to understand text, but they are a way to understand people." It is this kind
of conflict resolution that we need to be encouraging in our classrooms,
and Socratic circles offer a tremendous opportunity to do so.

Community-Building Skills

In addition to learning how to approach a problem in a collaborative
manner, Socratic circles encourage students to be accepting of people,
opinions, and ideas that are different from their own. Socratic circles have
been effective with a wide variety of students representing high and low
ability, and a full range of racial, cultural, and socioeconomic backgrounds.
In fact, Socratic circles that offer demographic variety have been
successful in breaking down stereotypes and cliques of students. A
freshman student writes of appreciating that diversity:

> *In high school, it seems like so many things get in the way of people really
> knowing one another's thoughts and opinions. It's refreshing to have a
> diverse group of students come together and share their significant ideas
> in a civil manner. Socratic circles provide a secure and calm place to
> express real opinions and intelligence.*

It is the open, honest sharing of personal opinion and experience that
allows students to view all people as sources of discovery. As Tredway
(1996) suggests, Socratic circles "draw in students who are often less
participatory and allow the synthesis of knowledge, ideas and personal
meaning to take place in a structured and creative way" (p. 18).

In my own classroom I have witnessed the power that engaging in
Socratic circles can have for a group of students. The frequency of classroom disruptions, misbehavior, and uncooperative attitudes appears to
decrease. Socratic circles encourage a sense of community and family that
helps make the overall classroom experience more rewarding for students
and teachers alike. Through Socratic circles students begin to see each

other as viable, important individuals capable of improving the quality of thinking and experience of all involved, regardless of race or background.

CONCLUSION

For centuries now, we have proceeded with the idea that knowledgeable teachers should stand before their classrooms and deliver information to a collectively stoic group of passive learners. But as our nation and our culture continue to grow and change at exponential rates and as our jobs, our families, our lives, and our dreams become more and more diverse, perhaps it is time we shift our styles and theories of education to facilitate meeting a broader range of needs. More than fifteen years ago, Dennis Gray (1989) argued for this very idea:

> If employers, college officials, parents, and a self-styled "Education President of the United States" genuinely want high school students who can think, read, write, and continue to learn, no time could possibly be more propitious for rousing the schools from their intellectual coma through the introduction of seminars. (p. 23)

However, few changes are visible in the expansion of Socratic circles in public education, and, unfortunately, we are no more adaptive today than we were in 1989.

All of the top-down reform movements in education are overlooking one very important reality. Honest change comes from within. Our nation is lacking the fundamental skills necessary to adapt in a constantly changing world. But changing our overall educational system will offer little improvement for this problem. Change needs to occur at the classroom level. "Fundamental reform requires internal change and personal effort because it is doomed to fail if mandated by outside authorities. It must come from inside ourselves for it to change attitudes and make lasting impact" (Lambright 1995, p. 30). Answers to our problems and our concerns are at our fingertips, but we as classroom teachers must take the initiative and make those changes happen. The reasons for these changes are clear:

> [E]ducators and students must change internally. We must think critically, creatively, differently. We must listen carefully and think out loud. We must take responsibility for what we say, work in a team setting, and come to terms with diverse, ambiguous meanings. We must work to distinguish between dialogue and discussion, to hone the art of critical thinking while practicing true communication and gaining intellectual empowerment. We must change the traditional image of the teacher as

an all-knowing authority and the student as a blank slate. (Lambright 1995, p. 34)

Those images, those ideas, those practices must change within our classrooms, for no other entity is strong enough to get the job done.

For that change to have a chance, we must temper our more didactic styles of teaching with a more maieutic form. We must empower our students in Socratic dialogue and offer them opportunities to practice the skills and processes they will rely upon throughout the remainder of their lives. If we honestly seek to produce self-directed learners and holistic individuals, we must change our classrooms and embrace strategies such as the Socratic circle.

Perhaps these ideas are best expressed by Miranda:

Through our Socratic circles and the opportunity to express my views, I have gained more self-confidence and realized that not everyone thinks they are better than me. I have learned that perhaps society is not at such a loss to have our generation; everyone is capable of having a thoughtful and civilized conversation. And that is a great awakening for me.

Chapter 2

THE NUTS AND BOLTS OF SOCRATIC CIRCLES

DIALOGUE INSPIRED BY JOHNNY CASH'S "FOLSOM PRISON BLUES."

MEGAN: *So, what do you think the train symbolizes?*

EMILY: *His freedom. It's everything he doesn't have in prison, the ability to move around, all the fancy things he dreams about.*

JOSH: *That makes sense. It seems pretty simple and straight-forward.*

WILL: *What about the train whistle, though? It's mentioned twice in the song. That must be important.*

JOSH: *What do think it means?*

WILL: *I'm not sure. I just think it's important. It's mentioned in the last line of the second stanza and again in the last line of the last stanza. Both times it's mentioned it also talks about being depressed. There must be a reason.*

MEGAN: *Well, if the train is his dream of being free, maybe the whistle is the reminder that the dream can't come true. I can almost picture this guy sitting there in his cell dreaming of being free and then hearing a distant train whistle and thinking about how everyone else has his dream and he's stuck there in jail.*

JOSH: *Kind of like when you see something you want but you know you can't have it. Eventually it almost seems like it's taunting you, and you start to hate it because you can't have it.*

25

EMILY: *I don't think he hates it, though. I think he still wants it. That's why he "hangs his head and cries."*

WILL: *But why is the whistle "lonesome" in the last line? Whistles aren't lonesome.*

JOSH: *That's true.*

EMILY: *I think it's the idea of the whistle being a reminder again. That whistle jolts him out of his dream. The whistle isn't lonesome, he is. The whistle is out there on the train moving around. He's stuck in his jail cell, going nowhere.*

JOSH: *But it says, "Let that lonesome whistle blow my blues away." It sounds like the whistle makes him feel better, not worse.*

MEGAN: *But that whole last part is set up by "if they freed me from this prison." I think what he's saying is that while he's in jail, that whistle reminds him of being locked up, like it's part of the punishment. But if he ever makes it out of jail, for the rest of his life that whistle will remind him of being free in a good way. It will remind him to appreciate his freedom.*

True classroom discussion, true dialogue, should be an opportunity for students to share their own ideas, build knowledge based on prior information being applied to new situations, test out their own hypotheses and perspectives against those of their peers, and arrive at an answer that has been constructed through personal experience, critical thought, rhetoric, and discourse. The Socratic circle is one such method for making this lonesome-whistle dream a reality in the classroom.

In the simplest terms, Socratic circles are an in-class discussion that is focused upon a particular piece of text that students have spent time reading and analyzing. However, the nature and process of that discussion differs radically from the typical teacher-led, question-and-answer discussion. In a Socratic circle, students work cooperatively to construct meaning from what they have read and avoid focusing on a "correct" interpretation of the text. Student understanding emerges as the discussion progresses and is always open to revision. Students base their construction of meaning upon the connections they can make to what they already know and the ideas and opinions that are shared within their group. This cooperative creation then stands as meaning over which students have almost complete ownership. The input and suggestions of the teacher are simply promptings to continue the process of discourse and the search for meaning.

It is important to note that Socratic circles are not a form of classroom debate. "Debate" suggests that students are competing with one another to convince an outsider of the validity of their line of thinking. A Socratic circle has students working collaboratively to construct a common vision of truth and understanding that serves all members of the group equally. There is no concept of "winning an argument" in a Socratic circle; there is only the search for deeper and more thorough understanding.

Similarly, there are strong differences between discussion as a general principle and Socratic dialogue. Discussion seeks to resolve an issue or solve a problem; it begins with a clear goal or outcome in mind such as, "Today we are going to discover the meaning of this poem." If we think of the typical kinds of questions we ask in a classroom discussion, most have a single, correct answer, or at the very least a preferable answer the teacher is waiting to hear. In my own experience, classroom discussion usually meant one of two things: either wading through several answers until I heard the one I was looking for, or completely exhausting the potential answers students were willing to offer and then spoon-feeding the answer I had been hoping to hear. Neither of these situations is consistent with Socratic dialogue, which often has no specific goal or outcome in mind. Socratic dialogue is an exploration, a quest for understanding, that has no definite beginning or end. It is an expedition into human experience and understanding that, as background, can then serve students as they approach life and the world they live in. Socratic dialogue is not about answers and solutions; it is about accepting multiple perspectives on a certain topic and reexamining our own experiences and opinions in light of those perspectives.

Socratic circles offer a controlled, pedagogical strategy that can bring dialogue into our classrooms, a type of real-world, student-centered learning where the teacher acts only to keep the discussion moving forward, regardless of its direction. As students construct their dialogue and their meaning of the piece of text, they are activating prior knowledge, making connections, and synthesizing new schemata in their quest for understanding. It is the students—not the teacher—who guide and direct the focus of the conversation in a search for meaning, understanding, and knowledge.

The ritualistic structure of a Socratic circle is one that appears complex to participants at first, but ultimately that structure is what provides for the students' growth and ownership of the conversation. By the end of the very first implementation, students have mastered the basic format of a Socratic circle. This allows them to focus on the content that is being discussed and the validity and power of the questions and thoughts being shared among participants. Such a structure also greatly reduces issues of classroom management, as each and every student is engaged in the conversation and filling a role for the group.

The basic procedure for a Socratic circle is as follows:

1. On the day before a Socratic circle, the teacher hands out a short passage of text.

2. That night at home, students spend time reading, analyzing, and taking notes on the text.
3. During class the next day, students are randomly divided into two concentric circles: an inner circle and an outer circle.
4. The students in the inner circle read the passage aloud and then engage in a discussion of the text for approximately ten minutes, while students in the outer circle silently observe the behavior and performance of the inner circle.
5. After this discussion of the text, the outer circle assesses the inner circle's performance and gives ten minutes of feedback for the inner circle.
6. Students in the inner and outer circles now exchange roles and positions.
7. The new inner circle holds a ten-minute discussion and then receives ten minutes of feedback from the new outer circle.

There are many variations to the time limits of each aspect of Socratic circles, but maintaining the discussion-feedback-discussion-feedback pattern is essential. Once students have mastered the structure of the Socratic circle itself, modifications can be made according to content, focus, purpose, and so on.

STARTING THE SOCRATIC CIRCLES PROCESS

For teachers new to the idea of Socratic circles, the idea of transforming a classroom to facilitate this style of and approach to learning can be daunting. Many teachers who observe my students in a Socratic circle are amazed by what they are able to accomplish and the manner in which they accomplish it. Many, after the initial jaw-dropping period passes, ask, "How do you get your kids to do that?" The answer is not simple. Effective Socratic circles do not happen overnight; there is no magic inoculation to suddenly make students think, act, and perform at this level. But with practice and careful teacher preparation, the results can be duplicated. To prepare for effective Socratic circle instruction, teachers need to consider and understand the importance of three key areas: classroom climate, the teacher's role, and teaching students to prepare for high-quality dialogue.

ESTABLISHING A CLASSROOM CLIMATE CONDUCIVE TO SOCRATIC CIRCLES

If one had the ability to look down upon a Socratic circle in my classroom from above, he or she would see two concentric circles. The inner circle of students would be facing inward and seated upon the floor, each with a writing utensil and a copy of the selected piece of text being used as a springboard for discussion. The outer circle of students, also facing inward, would be seated in desks directly outside the inner circle, almost literally hanging on every word of the inner circle. One would quickly realize that the only conversation taking place is among the members of the inner circle and that outer-circle members are busy observing and jotting down notes about the inner circle's performance, all without saying a word. One would also notice the teacher sitting outside the inner circle, contributing questions or basic information only to keep the inner circle's discussion moving smoothly along.

After several minutes had gone by, the observer would notice the teacher stopping the inner circle's conversation and asking them to remain quiet while the teacher led the outer circle in a conversation to provide feedback on the inner circle's performance. One would see students in the outer circle looking at their notes and commenting on the strengths of the inner circle and offering suggestions for improvement. What might surprise the observer is that the comments of the outer circle would be focused not on the content of the inner circle but rather on the behavior the members of the inner circle exhibited during their conversation. After several minutes the two circles would switch places and the process would be repeated.

The classroom environment is perhaps the element most crucial to Socratic circle success, both in terms of the physical environment and in terms of the emotional climate. Socratic circles approach reading, discussion, and learning in a way that is unfamiliar to many students. The physical layout of the room and the emotional climate established by the teacher greatly affect a student's willingness to try something new.

The process of mutual inquiry asks that participants take risks by sharing ideas and opinions regardless of their known "truth." Students, like all human beings, are sometimes uncomfortable and unsure of themselves when sharing information about which they are uncertain. The fears of being proved wrong, being judged, and/or being scoffed at are very real. The effective Socratic circle leader accommodates and lessens these fears in the classroom. One of the clear necessities is seating students in a circle so that they all can see each other when they are in discussion. Neat, straight rows of desks will not be conducive to an open, free-flowing dialogue. Because students are asking questions of each other and sharing personal ideas and opinions based on a selection of text, eye contact and nonverbal engagement in the conversation are essential. This engagement makes students more confident and comfortable, which makes them more likely to take risks in sharing their ideas. Ultimately, having students be able to see and interact with one another builds cohesion, a necessary component in the collaborative construction of new learning.

I also have my inner and outer circles sitting on different planes of the classroom. I always have my inner circle sitting on the floor and my outer circle sitting in chairs directly behind them. This allows the outer circle to almost literally look over the shoulders of the students sitting in the inner circle. Because the outer circle is responsible for watching the behavior of the conversation taking place, they need to be able to clearly watch and observe not only the discussion but also the physical and nonverbal interactions among students. The tiered circles in my classroom help the inner and outer circles see more clearly not only the members of their own circle, but the members of the other circle as well. This helps students see how beneficial one circle can be for the other. Because they can see and interact with one another, there is an enhanced amount of teamwork and cooperation between the circles; both know they are engaged in a cooperative endeavor.

I have also found that altering the lighting in my classroom helps to improve students' comfort level. Because large banks of overhead fluorescent lights seem to transform a classroom discussion into something that feels more like a police station interrogation, I fill my classroom with alternative lighting (such as floor lamps or strings of holiday lights hung from the ceilings) on days we hold Socratic circles. The change in lighting relaxes and calms students and makes them more open to the exchange of ideas and dialogue. One of the side benefits to this practice is that they respond very quickly to the lighting change. They know instantly what the order of business is for the day, and they move into Socratic circle mode more quickly, more fully, and with more enthusiasm.

Like the effects of classroom lighting, the importance of the emotional climate of the classroom cannot be underestimated. Sharing personal reactions, connections, and interpretations of ideas and concepts can be difficult for people of any age. For this to occur, students must feel safe, comfortable, and confident with themselves and with one another. Before Socratic circles are even introduced, teachers should take the time to engage students in multiple classroom climate activities. The value and benefit of knowing one another's names, interests, and personalities is immense. We simply cannot work cooperatively with people we feel no connection with, especially in a Socratic circle setting, where each individual is expected to contribute to group understanding.

THE TEACHER'S PLACE WITHIN A SOCRATIC CIRCLE

The outside observer often erroneously concludes that the teacher's role in the Socratic circle process is to just sit back and watch the events of the class period transpire as a passive observer, possibly grading papers or catching up on administrative paperwork while students do all of the work. When one views a Socratic circle from the perspective of a participant, one realizes this is anything but the truth. Leading is perhaps one of the most challenging roles within the Socratic circle structure for a variety of reasons. First, teachers must be flexible, adaptable, and willing to move with the ebb and flow of the chosen course of student conversation. Second, the leader must be willing to do, at times, what is difficult for most teachers to do: turn most of the control of the conversation over to the students themselves by not contributing too much and keeping all comments to the barest of necessities.

Specifically, the teacher's role in the Socratic circle process is fourfold: (1) to select the text for discussion, (2) to keep the discussion of the inner circle focused and moving, (3) to direct the feedback of the outer circle, and (4) to assess and evaluate the individual student and group performances. When done well these four tasks appear to the outside observer to be effortless and seamless within the Socratic circle itself. However, they require conscious planning and effort on the part of the teacher and are often overlooked in terms of importance. Socratic circles are a powerful classroom tool when used consciously to supplement the scope and sequence of the curriculum. But, like any other strategy, they can be a detriment to student growth when used in a haphazard or inept manner.

Selecting Good Text

Selecting a high-quality piece of text that augments and expands the content the class is already exploring is crucial to the success of a Socratic circle. Texts can be chosen for their richness in ideas, presentation of an issue, or examination of values as they encourage open and thoughtful conversation. Material taken from literature, history, science, math, philosophy, or current events may constitute a Socratic circle selection. Likewise, nontraditional sources such as a piece of art, a selection of music, or even a philosophical question may work as meaningful text. Good text raises questions in the participants' minds, questions for which there are no prescribed right or wrong answers. In fact, one of the marks of a truly effective Socratic circle is when participants leave with more questions than they brought with them. It is the process of Socratic questioning that develops students' skills in looking at the world around them with an inquisitive eye and the intrinsic quest for understanding that many times transcends the need to have a correct answer.

By far the most important aspect of selecting a piece of text for a Socratic circle is aligning it with the curriculum the class is currently studying. This can be a difficult task when the teacher cannot accurately predict the direction any given group of students may take a given selection of text. For this reason alone, text for Socratic circles must be thoroughly planned and carefully considered before being handed to students. And although it is certainly true that teachers can use Socratic questioning to guide students to a desired destination, students often bring content to the dialogue the teacher has never considered, and sometimes, that direction or content changes the teacher's perspective on the piece of text itself.

Socratic circles should not be implemented without great forethought and planning. Haphazardly scheduling dialogue about a piece of text that is unconnected or irrelevant to the material students are learning can lead to fruitful dialogue and important learning, but generally students see these Socratic circles as less than successful. Students report that their learning is most greatly affected when the text selected for a Socratic circle is relevant to what is being learned and is meaningful to their own lives.

Searching out high-quality pieces of text and continuously keeping an eye open for relevant and thematically connected works can greatly improve student perception of the circle's purpose. Although the process and criteria for selecting text are elements of Socratic circles that students never directly see, they are crucial for creating viable learning opportunities.

Monitoring the Inner Circle

A second part of the teacher's role is to facilitate the conversation of the inner circle, perhaps one of the most challenging roles for most classroom teachers to play. Teachers should strive to interrupt the discussion of the inner circle as infrequently as possible. The teacher's job is to act as a facilitator or coach for the conversation, not as the conversation's leader. And this goes against most of the training classroom teachers have received. It goes against our nature *not* to be the center of attention. For example, if the discussion begins to drift off topic, the teacher might pose a Socratic question to the group to help refocus and stimulate additional conversation. Or if the direction of the conversation appears to be heading down a dead-end path, a teacher might pose a question that helps the group redirect and recover the nature of the conversation itself. Or if the comments of one student need to be clarified or repeated for the group's understanding, the teacher might assist in that endeavor. Teachers should not, however, appear to favor any one student's comments over those of another or dismiss the group's line of thinking or interpretation. Ultimately, the less the teacher participates, the more ownership, control, and investment students feel for the conclusions their conversation draws.

One of the keys to a successful Socratic circle is the ability to turn the guidance of the conversation and the ownership of the material over to the students. Again, this is not to say that teachers should take a backseat to the whims and desires of their students. Managing the conversation of the inner circle is the most demanding aspect of the teacher's role. Teachers must be flexible in allowing student voice in the discussion, yet firm in instilling in their students a desire to push beyond the simple answers and examine all issues more thoroughly and in more detail. More information on managing the conversation of the inner circle is included in Chapter 4.

Many teachers ask if the time limits on the discussions can be modified as needed. The answer is certainly. There is no mandate that says each circle's discussion must last exactly ten minutes. Nothing is more frustrating than to have to stop a Socratic circle when students are creating good dialogue. It is, however, advisable to let students know approximately how many minutes they will be discussing or observing before they begin. This keeps the groups on-task and moving through the material, rather than thinking their time is unlimited and moving at a more leisurely pace.

As students build experience with Socratic circles and become more comfortable with the process, teachers might want to extend the time limits of each discussion to allow them to explore their ideas more fully. However, in the early stages, as students are still learning the basics of dialogue and cooperative inquiry, it is advisable to keep the times rather short.

Teachers in schools with block scheduling have also found great success in using Socratic circles. With the extra time available they have been able to expand the length of time devoted to discussion, rotate the groups through each circle's role more than once, and create follow-up activities for when the Socratic circle is complete.

Socratic circles can be modified and adapted as teachers see fit and can work in any setting, regardless of time constraints. In fact, in my own practice the actual time of each discussion varies according to how well each group is doing and how much ground they have covered. Flexibility and adaptability are two strengths of the Socratic Circle process and can greatly assist teachers in leading discussion that promotes dialogue.

Directing the Conversation of the Outer Circle

A third aspect of the teacher's role in a Socratic circle is guiding the outer circle's feedback and constructive criticism on the behavior and performance of the inner circle. One of the simplest and most successful ways of accomplishing this is simply to go around the circle and ask for initial observations. Once each student has offered an observation, the teacher can highlight particular points made and ask the group to brainstorm and predict solutions to any obstacles or problems noted.

The feedback provided to the inner circle is absolutely crucial to the success of Socratic circles. The feedback offers instant evaluation of the inner circle's performance and allows the outer circle to witness and study the performance of their peers in an endeavor they will be undertaking as well. The value and importance of such instant feedback should not be overlooked or underestimated. The comments of the outer circle allow the inner-circle participants to reflect upon their own performance and complete a cycle of self-assessment and the establishment of goals for future conversations. The teacher asking each student in the outer circle to offer at least one observation also encourages students to participate. For many of the quieter students, breaking the ice in the outer circle instills in them the confidence to participate more freely when they enter the inner circle.

Obviously one of the major challenges to the teacher during the outer circle's discussion is making sure the criticism remains constructive. However, this challenge is less serious than many might believe. Students know that whatever criticism they offer to the first inner circle will become a major focus when the circles are reversed. If Jackie points out that Alan has an annoying habit of tapping his pencil on the floor during the conversation, one can rest assured that Jackie's pencil will be the focus of attention when her group becomes the inner circle. What makes the feedback of Socratic circles work so well is the students' understanding that all participants are working with the same problems and under the same conditions. Providing feedback is not a onetime, isolated event but an ongoing struggle for improvement, Socratic circle after Socratic circle. Students understand the collective and collaborative nature of the process and know that understanding and truth hinge on their ability to work as a team.

One of the easiest ways to encourage evaluation, especially in the first few Socratic circles, is to ask each student in the outer circle to rate the inner circle on a scale of one to ten. This simple form of assessment lessens the burden placed on the outer circle and provides the inner circle with instant and easy-to-understand feedback. Teachers can then expand upon this method by also having the outer circle justify those ratings with specific observations of the inner circle's performance. Some of my students have even volunteered to chart the ratings over time to show class growth and improvement. Additional information about leading the discussion of the outer circle is included in Chapter 5.

Assessment and Evaluation

The final aspect of the teacher's role in the Socratic circle process is the assessment and evaluation of individual students and the class as a whole. Whether informally or formally, the teacher should assess performance in some manner. Teachers may develop rubrics, offer written feedback on the selections of text students annotate, or complete a scorecard or map (see Chapter 8). Perhaps most important in the process, however, is that teachers give verbal feedback at the conclusion of each inner circle and at the conclusion of the activity as a whole. It is this feedback that helps students understand their level of achievement and proficiency in the Socratic circle process.

In many ways, the teacher's role in a Socratic circle is similar to that of a traffic cop at an intersection where the stoplight has ceased working. The role of the teacher and the traffic cop alike is to direct the flow of movement. Ultimately, the movement's direction and destination are up to the travelers themselves. Because the teacher's role in a Socratic circle is quite different than the teacher's role in a more traditional lesson, many teachers feel awkward in their first few Socratic circle experiences. With time, the process of leading this type of classroom dialogue becomes more and more comfortable, and the growth that can be seen in students spurs teachers on to more experimentation and professional learning.

Chapter 3

PREPARING FOR CLASSROOM DIALOGUE

DIALOGUE INSPIRED BY DAVE MATTHEWS BAND'S "ANTS MARCHING."

JACOB: *This song is pretty depressing. I don't like it.*

KAYLA: *Why do you say that?*

JACOB: *Look at the last line of the chorus: "Lights down, you up and die." It's like the whole song is telling you that nothing in life matters, that we're all going to die in the end anyway.*

MIKE: *That's true, but I think it's deeper than that. It's not so much that nothing in life matters, but that we need to appreciate the things we do have and not take them for granted.*

JACOB: *Great, the "seize the day" idea again. Like we haven't talked about that before. Does everything we read always have to boil down to that?*

JESSICA: *I don't know. I don't think so. I guess I read this one a little differently. It's not so much about appreciating what you have. It's about taking chances and not being afraid to be different. I mean, that's what the title seems to imply.*

KAYLA: *That's true. When you think of ants marching, you think of little armies of ants working together to get something done.*

MIKE: *Don't ants smell each other's footprints?*

KAYLA: *What?*

MIKE: *I'm serious. I think I read something about it somewhere. Ants know to follow each other because their feet leave behind some kind of a scent to kind of mark the trail for the others.*

JACOB: *Okay, so what does that have to do with the song?*

JESSICA: *Well, isn't that kind of what each verse describes? In the first one, the man gets up, brushes his teeth, eats breakfast, and follows the same routine every day. In the second, he goes back to his mommy and she wipes away all of his fears. The image of the highway and all the cars following one another. It all seems to fit.*

MIKE: *But what about the candy man at the end?*

JESSICA: *Okay, so maybe it all doesn't quite fit perfectly. But it's starting to make more sense. All you have to do is add the word "if" to the chorus.*

KAYLA: *I can see that. But like Mike said, where does the candy man fit in? It seems like there has to be something more there.*

JACOB: *Maybe we're thinking too much like ants. Maybe we're all too content to follow this line of thinking. Maybe we need to look at it in a different way.*

JESSICA: *Maybe so.*

Because classroom dialogue can look and feel different from the traditional classroom discussions students are accustomed to, helping students understand and prepare for it in the classroom can help them be more comfortable and find more value in the process. Like ants marching, students find comfort and familiarity in routine, and at times these routines can be both helpful and hurtful. By incorporating new elements into classroom activities that students are more familiar with, by discussing the characteristics of dialogue, and by using critical reading skills to thoroughly prepare the selection of text for dialogue, students will be more successful at creating high-quality, student-centered dialogue.

ADAPTING CLASSROOM ACTIVITIES TO ENCOURAGE DIALOGUE

An easy way to introduce the elements of classroom dialogue to students, perhaps even before introducing the process of Socratic circles, is to begin weaving those elements into other activities with which students are already familiar. Lectures, study guides, small-group work, reading introductory textbook material, and other activities can all be modified slightly to begin developing student understanding of and experience with classroom dialogue.

Many students enter our classrooms with the conviction that knowledge and understanding exist outside of ourselves and that it is the job of the teacher, or some other expert, to dispense that knowledge and understanding to students. Whether it is the teacher disseminating information through a lecture or study guide or an outside expert providing information in a written or oral form, some students believe this passive style of learning is their only educational option. Because classroom dialogue requires students to engage with the material, finding ways to add more active student involvement to our lectures, study guides, video viewing, and so on can smooth the transition to more student-guided classroom dialogue.

I have used the four activities outlined below with great success to help students begin to see how their own questions and their own thinking can be great assets in any learning situation. Like effective prereading activities that preview material, activate prior knowledge, and establish a context for learning, these activities help students engage their critical thinking and establish a purpose for learning. In doing so, students not only become more active but also feel as though they are guiding more of their own learning, which is critical for effective dialogue.

Identifying Questions to Be Answered

One of the easiest extensions of an activity that can lay groundwork for more effective dialogue is a modification of the Know, Want to Know, Learned (KWL) prereading strategy. Before a lecture, a study guide, a video, or other classroom activity in which students tend to be more passive, I begin by having them generate a short list of questions they hope the activity will answer for them. I encourage students to ask as many open-ended questions as closed questions and focus on broad, general ideas rather than specific, factual information. Even when completing a worksheet or study guide, students are able to generate questions that help them connect the activity to their learning.

These questions can be created individually or in small groups, take only two to three minutes of class time, and help students predict the content to be explored. But because students are posing these predictions in the form of questions, their minds will naturally listen for potential answers. In my classes I have noticed that during a lecture or other activity, these questions encourage students to be more involved and participate more in what we are doing. Typically, students generate questions that focus as much on themselves as they do on the content. For example, a student may ask, "What am I going to gain from this video that will help me on next week's test?" or "What ideas will be discussed in the lecture that I might be able to use in my essay on the novel?"

A natural phenomenon occurs when students encounter a partial answer to their question and ask for clarification or further explanation. Sometimes I choose to answer these questions myself and sometimes I encourage other students in the class to address the question. Through this activity students learn that they can discover answers to their questions about the material by sharing those questions with others. Indirectly, students learn that answers to their questions are often more open to interpretation than they might have thought and that other students can be of great assistance in exploring those answers.

The familiar structure of these activities reassures students that asking their own questions and exploring the questions of others is safe and productive in terms of their own learning and growth.

Asking Further Questions

After an activity where students began by establishing questions to guide their learning, I finish by reviewing their original questions and the potential answers they discovered, and asking them to consider whether or not there are additional or follow-up questions that might be asked.

Having students share their questions and the answers they encountered can be productive for several reasons. First, students have a chance to rephrase their questions and summarize the information they found, which offers them a chance to reprocess the information and enables the rest of the class to hear it repeated in a voice other than that of the teacher or experts. This can be effective in helping students fully assimilate information. Second, students see examples of other students posing questions and exploring possible or partial answers. Very rarely are open-ended questions answered with absolute certainty, and students begin to see that partial answers are more favorable than no answers. They also see their peers struggling with questions and answers in ways that are similar to their own struggles. Last, in explaining the answers discovered, students often mention the comments and contributions made by other people in the class, reinforcing the collaborative process and search for understanding.

Discussing the questions students asked of themselves and the answers they discovered can take only a few minutes or considerably longer. For a particularly engaging activity or content, class-period-long discussions of questions and answers can ensue if time is available. However, asking one or two students to share their questions and answers can be equally effective and reinforce the skills that facilitate good dialogue.

I always conclude the activity by asking students to generate one or two additional questions that arose either because of the content presented or as the student considered and weighed information while attempting to answer another question. This reinforces to students the power and importance of questions and helps instill in them a sense of curiosity about the content of the activity. These follow-up questions are not explored directly in class but serve as a reminder that questions about any given topic can rarely be completely extinguished and that some will linger without answers. Although answerless questions can be frustrating to some students, classroom dialogue often generates questions that cannot be answered decisively or that are left open to personal interpretation. Experience with this reality before engaging in dialogue can reduce the temptation to abandon dialogue entirely.

Encouraging Multiple Perspectives

Another important skill students often feel less than comfortable with is embracing multiple perspectives on a given issue or topic. Helping students understand differing points of view and tolerate the ambiguity those views sometimes create can assist them in suspending judgments until they explore a topic more fully. In classroom dialogue this skill is important, because students without this ability sometimes arrive at conclusions too quickly, eliminating from their minds other productive avenues of discussion.

Again, working short extensions into other classroom activities can help students develop this skill and be more comfortable with its use. In my classes, I sometimes begin an activity with a statement related to its content that elicits a variety of opinions. With the instructions that there is to be absolutely no talking or discussion, I ask students to move to different corners of the classroom that represent the degree to which they agree or disagree with the statement. Once students have moved into their respective groups, I give them two minutes to discuss the statement and generate a list of three to five reasons for their position without interacting with any of the other groups.

Once they have compiled their short lists, I ask one member of each group to transfer theirs onto the chalkboard. Again, with the instructions that there is to be no discussion at this point, I review the points on each list for the class and ask students to raise a hand if there is an item whose surface meaning is unclear. Students are not to raise their hands if they disagree or think the logic expressed is faulty, but only if they find the item's meaning is unclear. If an item is unclear, I allow one student from the group to explain it to the class. This helps students consider and tolerate a wide range of positions and opinions.

The activity, whether a lecture, study guide, video, or something else, continues as originally planned, and the lists remain on the chalkboard throughout. When the activity is complete, I have students silently review the lists on the board. Then I ask for a show of hands from those who think their personal opinions are better represented by a list other than that of the group to which they originally belonged. I ask a few of them to share with the class their reasons for changing their opinions and how the content of the activity influenced that change. We discuss how important it is to be open to multiple points of view until we have examined all the information at hand, and how prejudging can lead us to choose not to examine information that has the potential to expand our understanding and possibly change our perspective. Of course, some students' opinions will not have changed by the end of the activity, but usually at least a few have.

A variation of this activity that requires less class time is to have students individually rate their levels of agreement on a scale of one to ten and list reasons for their ratings. After the activity, students review their reasons for the rating and raise their hands if they choose to change their original ratings. Again, students can discuss why they changed their ratings and the importance of considering multiple points of view before making a judgment.

Buzz Groups

A final activity that is useful in preparing students for classroom dialogue is one I have borrowed from Stephen Brookfield and Stephen Preskill's *Discussion as a Way of Teaching* (1999) known as buzz groups. This involves breaking students into small groups to address a short list of questions centered on the content of the day's activity. Brookfield and Preskill describe a buzz group as "usually made up of three or four students who are given a few minutes once or twice during a lecture to discuss a question or an issue that arises" (p. 48). Although described by the authors only as being used in a lecture, buzz groups are adaptable to the viewing of a video or as a reading activity.

The questions or issues that buzz groups address should be open-ended and allow students to think critically and speak persuasively about the material that has been presented, often taking a stand or making judgments about an idea's value or worth. Brookfield and Preskill offer examples of such questions:

• What's the most contentious statement you've heard so far in the lecture today?
• What's the most important point that's been made in the lecture so far?
• What question would you most like to have answered regarding the topic of the lecture today?

- What's the most unsupported assertion you've heard in the lecture so far?
- Of all the ideas and points you've heard so far today, which is most obscure or ambiguous to you? (p. 48)

Questions can also be created that are more specific to the content being presented or more relevant to upcoming assignments. Once students have participated in several buzz groups with questions proposed by the teacher, they can participate in more informal buzz groups in which they are responsible for generating and discussing their own questions.

The benefit of these buzz groups is that students are allowed an opportunity in a small group to begin discussing material and making judgments about its value and relevance. Working in small groups of three or four allows them to grow more comfortable sharing their opinions with peers and working together to make value judgments. They gain experience in thinking and speaking persuasively with the group, using evidence from the activity to support their positions. Buzz groups give students the opportunity to practice in small groups the skills needed for effective whole-class dialogue.

Learning to explore questions, embrace multiple perspectives, and support ideas with evidence are skills important to creating classroom dialogue and in having students think dialogue is productive and purposeful. By incorporating these elements into other classroom activities before engaging in dialogue, students will be more comfortable and effective in applying them and become more active and responsible for guiding their own learning.

DISCUSSING CLASSROOM DIALOGUE WITH STUDENTS

For decades now most classroom discussions have operated in a very similar manner. A teacher stands in front of a group of students (usually seated at desks arranged in straight rows) and poses a question to engage their minds. Students contemplate the question, one or two offer a possible answer, and then the teacher dispels the erroneous possibilities they offer, imparts the correct answer to the class en masse, and transitions to the next question.

In these traditional classroom discussions, teachers are exerting too much power, control, and voice in the conversation by being the entity that not only asks the questions but also provides what students view as the ultimate answers. The latent message of this practice is dangerous; students know full well that if they endure the discussion long enough, the teacher will provide the "correct" answer, which they can simply regurgitate onto a multiple-choice test or in an essay. By definition, a "discussion" suggests that ideas are being shared, that varying points of view and opinions are being accommodated, and that each participant walks away from the conversation having broadened her own horizons and expanded her thinking. Instead, because of the demands of behavior control and time management, classroom discussions have become modified lectures, thinly veiled in shadowy illusions of political correctness and etiquette.

Classroom dialogue, however, is inherently different from classroom discussion. In fact, when we think about the nomenclature surrounding the ideas of discussion and dialogue, we notice striking differences. A discussion is something we "hold" or "schedule"; it is a meeting of a group of people where a subject is considered in hopes that some "conclusion" or "resolution" can be reached. Discussion is a *deductive* process by which we move from many ideas at the beginning to markedly fewer ideas at the end. In the classroom, we may hold a discussion on the essay topics assigned for a particular piece of literature. As teachers we offer further explanation beyond what is written on the page, answer questions, and clear up areas where students are unclear or confused. We know this discussion is over when we have reached the point where students have no more questions and appear comfortable and able to begin working. We have reached a conclusion; all parties involved are "on the same page" and ready to proceed with the assigned task.

Dialogue, on the other hand, is much more philosophical in nature. We "open" a dialogue, rather than "holding" or "scheduling" one; we seek to illuminate an issue or an idea that incorporates many opinions and many points of view in hopes of "expanding" and "broadening" our knowledge and understanding. It is an *inductive* process by which we increase the number of ideas as our conversation moves forward. In the classroom, the early stage of brainstorming for a piece of writing is a type of internal dialogue. We begin by generating ideas, often writing down as many as we can think of, unsure of which ones we may need later and which we may not. We weigh and consider new thoughts and alternatives that come into our brains, adapting and modifying the ideas that existed before. What frustrates so many of us about this process is that we may never feel we have reached a conclusion; in fact, there may not be a conclusion. Later in the writing process—perhaps even in the stages of revising and editing—we may find ourselves slipping back into the realm of brainstorming, weighing and considering new ideas we had not contemplated before. With dialogue, "conclusion" and "resolution" may never appear.

Helping students understand the difference between dialogue and discussion can be of great assistance in breaking the mold of traditional classroom discussions. Some students, however, may still resist making the transition from teacher-focused to student-focused conversations. For those students, the control and direction the teacher provides those conversations is a comfortable security blanket. These behaviors can greatly improve students' willingness to test the waters of more student-centered dialogue.

Another successful manner in which to prepare students for classroom dialogue before engaging in Socratic circles is simply to discuss the process and its benefits with them. More and more students have encountered the term "Socratic circle" or have heard accounts of participation in them from others. Although this may not take much class time and may be a onetime event, tapping into some of the preconceived ideas and allowing a forum for students to share their interests, apprehensions, and even fears about Socratic circles can help them become more comfortable with the process.

Reflective Letters from Previous Students

One of the successful techniques that I have used to help alleviate student fears and misconceptions is to share with them letters written by previous students reflecting on their Socratic circle experience. Many times apprehensions are best relieved by peers, and helping students see beyond the issues that trouble them can improve the overall Socratic circle experience.

Typically, toward the end of the semester or school year I ask students to compose a letter addressed to future students in the same class that explains their growth through our experience with Socratic circles. Students who felt apprehensive about the experience generally write very openly and honestly about those fears and how they became more comfortable with the Socratic circle process once they realized those fears were unfounded. More important, the letters typically report the tremendous growth students have seen in their own development and learning. These letters not only make for high-quality summative assignments, but also can help subsequent students keep an open mind about classroom dialogue. Figure 3.1 represents the kind of letter students typically write.

With student permission, I keep several of these letters from each class and distribute them to students in subsequent years. I arrange students in small groups, then ask each group to read over their handful of letters and record information on a three-column chart. In one column students identify the apprehensions and fears the letter writers had before beginning Socratic circles, a second column records the benefits students perceived through participating in them, and the third column reports drawbacks to the activity. Once students have charted this information, most quickly see that former students found great value in Socratic circle participation and that the vast majority of their apprehensions were unfounded.

FIGURE 3.1 Dear
Future Student . . .
letter

Dear Future Student,

Over the course of the next year, you will have the privilege of participating in Socratic circles. These interactive tutorials served as more than a mere stepping-stone in the maturity of my writing, and I know they can do the same for you.

As a freshman in a big, new school, I'll admit the idea of Socratic circles was a little intimidating at first. Sharing ideas and asking questions with maybe one night of preparation? Not to mention the fear associated with speaking during class if you are one of those individual learners like me. I thought the requirement of adding to the discussion would be the death of me and my English grade. Turns out, the more Socratic circles you do, the easier it becomes to analyze with and even without your class.

I cannot encourage you enough to speak out your ideas and questions, even if you think they sound rather ridiculous. Some of the best conversations have sprung from the most random and presumably easy questions.

There will be no end to the lessons you gain by Socratic circles if you are open to them. Socratic circles have taken my literary interpretations to depths I was not expecting to reach. So not only do they create a comfortable environment for you to share your opinions and become acquainted with your classmates; they also staggeringly enhance an individual's ability of finding meaning and symbolism in various works of art—two factors that will become essential in your high school English career.

If I had not had the experiences of Socratic circles as an initial aspect of high school English, I would be nowhere near prepared for the upcoming year. Take advantage of these Socratic circles; your writing and classroom assertion will reach new heights.

Examining Characteristics of Dialogue and Debate

After we talk about the reflective letters of previous students, I engage in a short discussion of the characteristics of dialogue and contrast them with the characteristics of debate. One of the most prevalent misconceptions students have about Socratic circles is that they are a form of competitive debate in which participants argue to win. This can be destructive to the quality of classroom dialogue, because dialogue represents the collaborative quest to construct knowledge.

Using the chart represented in Figure 3.2 and taken from Saskatchewan Education's Curriculum Guide for "Law 30: The Law and You," I discuss with each of my classes the characteristics of dialogue as opposed to those of debate. By talking through each of these points, students begin to see how different the two forms of communication are and how crucial the ideas of collaboration and teamwork are for effective classroom dialogue.

PREPARING FOR SOCRATIC CIRCLE DIALOGUE

Once students have been exposed to and discussed the various elements of classroom dialogue, we spend time preparing for actual Socratic circle

Dialogue	Debate
Dialogue is collaborative. Two or more sides work together toward common understanding.	Debate is oppositional. Two sides oppose each other and attempt to prove each other wrong.
In dialogue, finding common ground is the goal.	In debate, winning is the goal.
In dialogue, one listens to the other side(s) to understand, find meaning, and find agreement.	In debate, one listens to the other side to find flaws and to counter its arguments.
Dialogue enlarges and possibly changes a participant's point of view.	Debate affirms a person's own point of view.
Dialogue complicates positions and issues.	Debate simplifies positions and issues.
Dialogue reveals assumptions for reevaluation.	Debate defends assumptions as truth.
Dialogue causes introspection on one's own position.	Debate causes critique of the other position.
It is acceptable to change one's position.	It is a sign of weakness and defeat to change one's position.
Dialogue is flexible in nature.	Debate is rigid in nature.
Dialogue stresses the skill of synthesis.	Debate stresses the skill of analysis.
Dialogue opens the possibility of reaching a better solution than either of the original solutions.	Debate defends one's own position as the best solution and excludes other solutions.
Dialogue strives for multiplicity in perspective.	Debate strives for singularity in perspective.
Dialogue affirms the relationship between the participants through collaboration.	Debate affirms one's own strength in opposition to other points of view.
Dialogue creates an open-minded attitude, an openness to change.	Debate creates a close-minded attitude, a determination to be right.
In dialogue, one submits one's best thinking, knowing that other people's reflections will help improve it rather than destroy it.	In debate, one submits one's best thinking and defends it against challenges to show that it is right.
Dialogue calls for temporarily suspending one's beliefs.	Debate calls for investing wholeheartedly in one's beliefs.
In dialogue, one searches for basic agreements.	In debate, one searches for glaring differences.
In dialogue, one searches for strengths in the other position.	In debate, one searches for flaws and weaknesses in the other position.
Dialogue involves a real concern for the other person and seeks to not alienate or offend.	Debate involves a countering of the other position without focusing on feelings or relationship, and often belittles or deprecates the other position.
Dialogue assumes that many people have pieces of the answer, and that together they can put them into a workable answer.	Debate assumes there is a right answer and that someone has it.
Dialogue encourages depolarization of an issue.	Debate encourages polarization of an issue.
In dialogue, everyone is part of the solution to the problem.	In debate, one person or viewpoint wins over the other.
Dialogue affirms the idea of people learning from each other.	Debate affirms the idea of people learning individually in competition with others.
Dialogue remains open-ended.	Debate implies a conclusion.

FIGURE 3.2 Dialogue vs. Debate chart ("Comparison of Dialogue and Debate" reprinted with permission of Saskatchewan Learning, Regina, Saskatchewan, Canada)

participation. Effective Socratic dialogue is dependent upon all participants doing a close, critical reading of the selection of text being discussed. In addition to teaching students how to annotate text and generate questions to be used in dialogue, I motivate them to prepare for each Socratic circle and carefully manage those who are reluctant to prepare.

Preparing the Text

A Socratic circle is only as successful as the work put into preparing for it. Students and teachers alike must spend time, effort, and energy training their minds to look for the intricacies that reading, thinking, and discussing require. A teacher's job preparing for each Socratic circle involves selecting text, contemplating the connections that can be made to the curriculum being studied, and generating potential questions to help elicit good dialogue from students. But before any of this can take hold and be considered a worthwhile investment of time, teachers must also train students to read actively, read responsively, and think both critically and creatively.

Obviously, encouraging and helping students to prepare is essential in the dialogue process, and at the heart of that preparation is close and critical reading of the selection of text. Students who have not read and thought about the topic and the context of what has been written or created will generate nothing but the most superficial of ideas in discussion. Therefore teaching students a systematic method for annotating the text they read is often highly successful in helping them prepare for a Socratic circle.

Early in the process, students may not see the value and purpose of annotating text in helping them prepare for classroom dialogue. Too many of our students view reading as a passive, complacent activity. They assume that skimming the rows of typeset letters will suffice to absorb, contemplate, and understand the material and the point the writer is making. As teachers, we know this is not the case, and we must show our students that true reading involves much more work on their part than they would believe.

To show students the kind of interaction that should occur between writer and reader I use an analogy that I have adapted from Mortimer Adler. In my classes, I compare the interaction between a writer and a reader to that of a pitcher and a catcher in baseball. When I ask my students whether the pitcher or catcher is more important in a baseball game, they usually jump to answer the pitcher. Students view the pitcher as the player doing the work—selecting the pitch, determining its position over the plate, and, of course, throwing the ball. In student minds, the catcher is simply a passive receiver who mindlessly throws the ball back to the mound in anticipation of the next pitch. But when I ask my students to imagine the repercussions in a baseball game in which a pitch was made and a catcher was not present, they quickly begin to see that the catcher is an integral part of the process and that without someone behind the plate, the game could not continue. We then discuss how catchers sometimes question pitch selection with signals, and how they are responsible for monitoring the movement of base runners and even, at times, motivating the pitcher and calming his nerves. After discussing these points, students see that the pitcher and the catcher are equally important. We then compare this relationship to that of writer and reader.

When I ask my students whether a writer or a reader does more work, they typically jump to the conclusion that the writer, like the pitcher, is the more active participant. It is the writer who selects topics, chooses manners and methods to express ideas, and does the work of presenting the material to the reader. On the other hand, the reader, like the catcher, sits behind home plate to passively absorb the thoughts the writer has put on paper. I explain to my students that if they read in a passive manner, they are as destructive to the game of written communication as a passive catcher who does nothing but act as a mechanical ball-return device behind the plate is to a baseball game. We discuss the idea that like good catchers, good readers must take on a more active role. They must question what is coming next, question delivery, manage the ideas the writer has left circulating on the field of play, and, at times, provide feedback that motivates or calms the nerves of the writer. With this analogy students quickly begin to see that reading is a much more active process than they once thought.

Once students are convinced that high-quality reading requires just as much energy, work, and effort as high-quality writing, we begin talking about methods of documenting that mental work. For the writer, the fruits of his or her labor are right there on the page, but for the reader, the vast majority of work that takes place is mental, and unable to be seen by an outside observer. To make that mental work more visible and document the thinking that has occurred, I teach my students how to annotate text.

As Carol Porter-O'Donnell (2004) describes, annotating text "helps readers reach a deeper level of engagement and promotes active reading" while making a "visual record of the thoughts that emerge while making sense of the reading" (p. 82). Annotations may include predictions, opinions, reflections, connections, and—most important for Socratic circles—questions. Claggett, Reid, and Vinz (1998) refer to this idea as "having a conversation with the words on the page" (p. 10) and suggest students consider completing five tasks while reading:

1. circling any vocabulary words students are unfamiliar with or would
    have difficulty explaining to others
2. underlining key phrases
3. keeping track of the story or idea as it unfolds
4. noting word patterns and repetitions or anything that strikes the
    student as confusing or important
5. writing down questions in the margins

Typically, my students leap right into this strategy and can fill the
margins of a page with their annotations. For some students, however,
annotating is more difficult, especially the questions. This most often
stems from years of reading passively rather than actively. In almost every
class when we first explain and practice annotating text, I have one or
more students who claim that when they read, no questions arise in their
minds. For some students this is because they are simply moving their eyes
over the text without truly contemplating the meaning and message of
what is being written. Other students don't write down questions because
they feel embarrassed by the ones they do have. Unintentionally, we teach
students at an early age that having questions suggests a lack of understanding, rather than suggesting that having questions reveals a curiosity
for further learning.

I suggest to these students that perhaps they have no questions about the
text because they haven't truly read it, that they are not fully processing the
ideas being described. I then explain that they will know when they are truly
reading because questions about the text will explode in their minds like fireworks, and that they should read and reread as many times as it takes to make
those questions arise. We then discuss the importance of jotting down as
many of those questions as the hand can manage, without thought to their
quality. In an actual Socratic circle, those questions become a warehouse of
ideas. The more questions written down, the more potential lines of conversation can take place, thereby improving the quality of the dialogue.

In class we practice annotating text both before I introduce Socratic
circles and after we have progressed through two or three conversations.
Once students have experienced a Socratic circle or two, they better
understand the purpose and context of annotating text and benefit from
reexamining how it is done. To practice I typically hand students a selection of text and allow them ten minutes or so to annotate, spurring them
on to fill the page as much as possible with their annotations. A crucial
next step is to have them share their annotations in small groups so that
they can compare their own ideas to those of their fellow students.
Quickly students realize that there is not necessarily a right or wrong way
to annotate text and that opinions expressed by one student may be
completely different from those expressed by another.

As students share their annotations in small groups and compare methods of annotating, I circulate around the room, randomly holding up examples so the whole class can observe and study the different styles. This helps to model examples of the strategy and reinforce the process in students' minds. Over the last couple of years I have been amazed at some of the inventive methods students have come up with for annotating text. Some choose to color-code their annotations, using colored pencils to mark vocabulary words in one color, identify key phrases in another, and so on. Other students choose to code their annotations graphically, drawing large question marks next to areas of the text that inspire questions, small cameras next to passages that incorporate a great deal of visual imagery, and so on. Still other students prefer to write their annotations on a separate sheet of paper in the form of a dialectical journal (Berthoff 1987). In this method, they create a two-column chart in which they quote the text in the left-hand column and offer their annotations in the right-hand column. (Figures 3.3 and 3.4 represent how different students annotate text in different ways.) I typically leave the specific method of annotating text up to the individual student; over time, each student develops the technique that works best for him or her. I do reinforce with each text we annotate, however, that the annotations are our only way of documenting each student's preparation and that better-prepared participants lead to better classroom dialogue.

To ensure that students are well prepared for each Socratic circle, some of my colleagues use each student's annotations as an "admission ticket" to the activity itself. Students who are not prepared with annotations for the text before the conversation are asked to sit in the back of the room until they can show that their critical reading has been completed and they are prepared for dialogue with others.

Preparing Students

Even before a Socratic circle starts, teachers must work hard to establish a climate and context in his or her classroom that will make the inner-circle dialogue successful. Motivating students and preparing them both academically and socially for the process greatly affects the final product.

Thorough preparation on the part of students before engaging in a Socratic circle is an absolute must for valuable dialogue to occur. Poor preparation typically leads to conversation that lacks organization, insight, and relevance to the material the teacher hopes students will learn. With this in mind, it is crucial to help students understand *how* to prepare for a Socratic circle and to understand *why* preparing for it is important.

However, there are times when, because of a wide range of possible reasons, students may not be prepared. Some of the reasons may be partic-

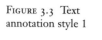

FIGURE 3.3 Text annotation style 1

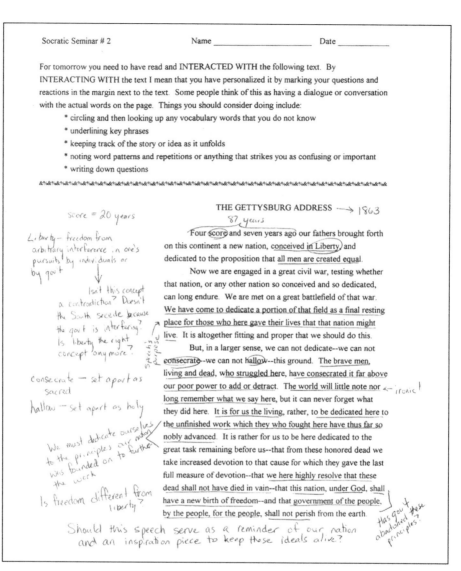

ular to individual students—such as an inability to connect with the text, lack of access to a dictionary or other reference materials, or a lack of sleep—whereas other obstacles may plague any number of students, such as difficulty of the text, a topic too close to their personal lives, or a conflict with an important basketball game the night before. Regardless of the reasons for the lack of preparation, teachers must make accommodations and adapt their plans accordingly. Attempting to force dialogue when adequate preparation has not taken place is counterproductive to the process and reinforces in student minds that Socratic circles are nothing but glorified bull sessions.

"Address to the Joint Session of Congress and the American People" September 20, 2001 — President George W. Bush	
"enemies of freedom"	Is it really proper to believe this nonsense? That the US is the only "free" country? These are enemies of the US, hence the reason they didn't attack Britain
"different world"	It is a powerfully delivered speech with an imperative feeling about his message, but is it propaganda? In retrospect, how much feeling of truth does it provide
"America makes the following Demands on the Taliban"	This is a bold and yet necessary statement
"they will share in their fate"	Good call. The Taliban fell.
"By sacrificing life to serve their radical visions - by abandoning every value except the will to power"	Very well stated. Although, this country's history is in violation of this (ie. Trail of Tears)
"in history's unmarked grave of discarded lies"	This is a poetically fantastic phrase (props to the speech writer)
"Either you are with us, or you are with the terrorists"	This has turned into a long campaign which once had its roots in a good cause - to bring to justice the 9/11 committers, but now the war has gone south and is no longer grounded in seeking justice but rather using its big stick as a police force.
"live your lives"	I bet there will be a draft. Does that mean the gov't will give me a new life to live?
"hug your children"	Yea. Do. Even if nothing happens - love fixes a lot of things wrong in the world
"fight for our principles"	Which so far have been bashed by the Patriot Act & other corresponding "big brother" legislation

Motivating students to engage in dialogue in the classroom can be particularly effective in two very different realms. For some students, knowing that the dialogue about to take place will better prepare them for assessment is important motivation. When they begin to see that the expansion and empowerment of their own thoughts and ideas can be enhanced through dialogue, many realize that it can help them generate content for writing assignments, both in paragraph responses on exams and in more formal essay assignments. Also, by connecting new learning to prior knowledge, dialogue can help prepare students for more standardized exam questions as well.

For students less concerned with their grades, dialogue can provide opportunities to relate learning to their personal lives. I sometimes relate a selection of text to an analogous situation in students' lives before our Socratic circle to encourage them to seek out those personal connections. For example, I preface our reading of A. E. Housman's "To an Athlete Dying Young" by asking students to think back over their lives to a situation or relationship that ended in a less than satisfactory manner. By having students discuss or briefly write about these experiences we establish personal connections to the text that draw our interest for the upcoming dialogue and help students see the relevance of the text to real-world situations. Like any lesson involving the reading of literature, prereading activities can be very successful in generating student enthusiasm and motivation for the Socratic circle process.

Another strategy I use at the beginning of the Socratic circle to help students refocus their minds on the reading is to ask for a volunteer to read the text out loud just before the first inner circle's conversation. This enables students to hear the piece in another person's voice, which sometimes influences and changes their interpretation of the piece, and gives them an opportunity to review the annotations they made the night before. This helps them organize and prioritize their thoughts one last time before engaging in classroom dialogue.

Of course, there are times when students are not adequately prepared for dialogue. For a teacher, these can be some of the most frustrating and infuriating moments in working with Socratic circles. Typically when students are collectively ill prepared, it becomes apparent to all involved within the first minutes of the inner circle's conversation. Student eyes fall to the text, or to their shoestrings, or to poking holes in their paper with their pencils. Many students frown in disappointment or smirk in embarrassment. At this moment the teacher must decide either to prompt the group with further questions to kick-start the conversation or postpone the activity and allow students more time to complete the reading and process their thoughts.

Either decision poses potential problems for the Socratic circle. Prompting the group with further questions can allow students to revert to their prior experience with teacher-led class discussions. Many students are more than happy to allow the teacher to guide the conversation and draw attention away from their embarrassment about their lack of preparation. In my experience, when this happens, everyone becomes frustrated with the lack of dialogue and the strategy fails to produce the desired results. Likewise, postponing the activity and allowing students more time to read and prepare for dialogue reinforces the idea that they can get by with little preparation the night before, and that can greatly harm the quality of Socratic circles over time.

The most successful strategy I have found in dealing with this situation is to simply cancel the activity for the day and continue with the class's other learning activities. This reinforces in student minds that adequate preparation is necessary and gives them time to prepare at home that night. Whether out of guilt or out of disappointment at being denied the opportunity for dialogue, students come back the next day prepared and ready to participate. In my years of using Socratic circles, I have never had to do this more than once with a class in a particular semester.

CONCLUSION

Activities designed to better prepare students for classroom dialogue make Socratic circles more productive and more fruitful for student learning. By working elements of dialogue into preexisting activities, students have a chance to develop the skills needed for effective dialogue and to grow more comfortable with them before Socratic circles begin. Thorough preparation and critical reading of each selection of text is also crucial. Engaging classroom dialogue through Socratic circles occurs only with the motivation and preparation of all stakeholders.

Chapter 4

FACILITATING THE INNER CIRCLE

DIALOGUE INSPIRED BY LANGSTON HUGHES'S "LET AMERICA BE AMERICA AGAIN."

JALEN: *What do you think the tone of this poem is?*

TARA: *It's hard to pin down. There's some anger in there, there's some regret, there's even some pride.*

CHRIS: *I agree. But more than anything I think the tone is hopeful and determined. The second to last stanza says it all, I think: "And yet I swear this oath— / America will be!" This guy is determined to make America a great place.*

ZACH: *What do you mean by a "great place"?*

CHRIS: *A place where freedom reigns. You know, land of the free, home of the brave kind of thing.*

ZACH: *Do you think that's what Langston Hughes means?*

CHRIS: *Yeah, don't you?*

ZACH: *I don't know. I mean, I see it on one level, but I think there's something more there, too. Something deeper.*

SAMANTHA: *Like what?*

ZACH: *On one hand he's being critical of America. He gives the examples of slavery, and Native Americans being forced from their lands, and poverty. He says, "America never was America to me." But on the other hand, it's like he's celebrating all of those things, too. Celebrating the fact that we've all survived them and we're still fighting for what we believe in.*

SAMANTHA: *So, you think he's trying to inspire the reader to keep reaching for that dream?*

ZACH: *Yeah.*

JALEN: *He's sure got a funny way of going about it.*

TARA: *What do you mean by that?*

JALEN: *I don't know. I guess if I were trying to convince people that America is this grand and glorious place where all of your dreams can come true, I'd give examples of people who had done just that. Not examples of the people who have suffered and not found what they were looking for.*

CHRIS: *But I think that's his point. Sure, some people have come to America and made their fortune and been successful and made all their dreams come true. But until we all reach that place, until we start helping each other achieve our dreams, America will never live up to the hype of what it was made out to be.*

TARA: *I think that's a really good point, but he keeps referring to "making America be America again," like at some point in our history we did help each other reach our dreams but now we're not.*

ZACH: *Can you think of any times in our history when we were like that?*

TARA: *I can't. And like Jalen said, don't you think he would offer examples of times when this stuff did happen if he wanted to motivate us to keep working for it?*

JALEN: *Maybe that's why he leaves the example so generic by just using the word "again." He mentions the word "again" and we all start thinking in our own minds about those good times in our pasts. They're probably different for every one of us, and the simple word "again" kind of triggers those more personal memories.*

SAMANTHA: *I don't think I get it.*

ZACH: *I get it. He kind of dangles our own successes in our faces and contrasts them with the struggles of all of these others. Kind of a subtle and sneaky way to encourage us to work together and help each other reach all of our dreams.*

Once students are prepared for dialogue, the class is ready to begin the Socratic circle process, guiding one another on an intellectual journey within the inner circle on the path toward enlightenment and understanding. And like the dialogue above, that journey is often built upon previous successes and the desire to lift others to similar heights. The teacher's job at the beginning of the Socratic circle is to randomly divide the class into two groups and offer an initiating question to focus the inner circle's approach to analyzing the text and starting their dialogue.

DIVIDING THE CLASS INTO CIRCLES

The event that launches the Socratic circle is randomly dividing the class into two, fairly equal-sized groups. This also gives students a moment to gather their materials and themselves and move into their respective circles. After the initial Socratic circle, when the rules and the process are explained in detail, the division and movement can be completed quickly, typically taking no more than ten to twenty seconds.

There are no right or wrong ways to divide the class into two circles. Generally, I divide the class in such a manner that groups are unpredictable and random. Students should not be able to predict which circle they will be in or whether they will be in the first or second inner circle. To accomplish this I ask the class a question with only two possible answers and allow the answers themselves to dictate the membership of each group. For example, I might say, "What month of the year were you born? If you were born in the months January through June, please move to the inner circle, and if you were born in the months July through December, please move to the outer circle." This method offers a quick and easy way to randomly divide the class into two groups. Figure 4.1 lists other questions teachers have used to create their circles.

Of course, I am not checking ID cards to verify birth dates as students are forming their circles. And I am sure there are times when, for whatever reasons, students fib to be in one particular circle rather than the other. For the most part, however, I let this go. The circles themselves and the particular students in them are not the focus of the activity. If I see a particular student, or more likely a small group, who appears to be attempting to dictate which circle he, she, or they will be in, and I think it could have a detrimental effect on the dialogue, I ask particular students to switch groups.

Likewise, there are times when my "random" questions do not produce groups that are quite as random as I would like. Sometimes one group will have noticeably more people than the other, or one sex or race will be over-represented. As students divide themselves into their respective circles, I watch carefully and observe the general makeup of each circle. And at times, I ask certain students to move into the other circle to balance numbers or the backgrounds they represent. In the back of my mind is the idea that the circles of each Socratic circle should be as heterogeneous as possible.

Another challenge that develops as students move into their circles is the breaking of habits. Like all human beings, students tend to habitually sit in the same location or next to the same person when possible. Habits such as these can influence behavior and ultimately the quality of the dialogue. For example, two students who are very good friends may sit next to each other in the inner circle. Because of their close friendship,

Student Attributes	Student Preferences
Males / Females	Beach vacation / Ski vacation
Long hair / Short hair	Dogs / Cats
Last name A-L / Last name M-Z	Delivery / Carry-out
Pants / Shorts	Vanilla ice cream / Chocolate ice cream
Socks / No socks	Professional sports / College sports
Glasses / No glasses	Acoustic guitar / Electric guitar
Long sleeves / Short sleeves	Reading / Writing
Shoes / Sandals	Fruits / Vegetables
Hat / No hat	Car / Pickup
Odd last digit of phone number / Even last digit	Rainy days / Snowy days
Jan.-June birthday / July-Dec. birthday	Carnivore / Herbivore
Watch / No watch	Bath / Shower
Green or blue eyes / brown or hazel eyes	MTV / VH1
T-shirt / Other shirt	Leno / Letterman
Born in the first half of the month / Born in the second half of the month	Hamburgers / Pizza
Shirt with a collar / Shirt without a collar	Cook / Clean
Light-colored shoes / Dark-colored shoes	Water ski / Snow ski
Visual learners / Auditory learners	Math and science classes / English and history classes
Introverts / Extroverts	Music / Movies
Right brained / Left brained	Morning person / Night owl
Denim pants / Other pants	Spring / Fall
Light-colored hair / Dark-colored hair	Winter / Summer
Two or fewer siblings / More than two siblings	Elvis / The Beatles
Traveled out of the country / Haven't traveled out of the country	Toast / Bagel
Has pet / Does not have pet	

FIGURE 4.1 Breaking into Circles list

their comments may (probably unintentionally) be directed more to each other than to the entire circle. To combat these types of problems, I might ask particular students to switch places with others in the same circle. Although I use this technique only occasionally, it does help maintain the randomness of circle membership and student location within the circle.

Tinkering too much with the circles themselves can be just as much of a problem as a solution. I prefer to keep this aspect of Socratic circles as quick and simple as possible, making changes only when I think they will enhance the quality of the dialogue.

THE INITIATING QUESTION

Once the two circles are formed and students are in their places, it's time to begin the actual Socratic circle. Sometimes students have so many ideas and so many things they want to share with and ask of the group that they have no idea where to begin. Other students (particularly early in the morning) have difficulty waking their minds up, focusing on one particular area of the text, and launching the discussion. To help alleviate these problems and to help students get the ball rolling, I typically begin each circle with an initiating question. For example, when discussing William Stafford's poem "Traveling Through the Dark," I may offer the initiating question, "You'll notice the word 'swerve' is used in both the first and last stanza. What might Stafford be trying to get you all to think about by repeating this same idea twice in his poem?" This question helps focus student minds and offers a small chunk of common ground from which to begin their dialogue.

A good initiating question has several characteristics, among them specificity, being based in opinion, being focused on the meaning the writer is attempting to convey, and having the potential to elicit multiple answers that may conflict with each other. An overly general initiating question such as, What did you think of this piece? can cause more harm than good in a Socratic circle. Students can spend several minutes or perhaps even their entire allotted time discussing what they liked and disliked about the text and never progress into a more meaningful, analytical examination of the selection. Likewise, some initiating questions can be too specific, although this situation is much easier to accommodate. For example, some classes will discuss the initiating question above for "Traveling Through the Dark," and as soon as several students have shared their ideas, the conversation fizzles out. But by using a more general follow-up question, such as, Do any of you see other examples of words or ideas that are repeated in the poem?, the conversation recovers and continues. When constructing initiating questions I err on the side of over-specificity. Having a specific first question and a more general follow-up question leaves students with the feeling that they are being turned loose to explore the text. Beginning with a general initiating question and following up with a more specific question suggests to students that you are guiding and leading them through the text by the hand.

The vast majority of my initiating questions also focus on the meaning (or some aspect of the meaning) the writer is attempting to convey. I have found this to be successful in Socratic circles because it starts the conversation moving in a fruitful direction. Most of the time, students are aware enough to bring whatever ideas they are discussing back to the meaning being conveyed through the text in some manner. Focusing the initiating question on this meaning reinforces that this is the ultimate goal and establishes a stronger sense of purpose in their dialogue.

Finally, I also try to create open-ended initiating questions that will elicit multiple answers and reveal differing opinions and points of view. This is particularly helpful in creating an environment in which students understand that disagreeing is acceptable, healthy, and can often enhance understanding. Creating and asking such initiating questions allows the teacher to model for students constructive methods of responding to differing opinions. This helps to reduce the potential for problems later in the dialogue when students attempt to accommodate differences of opinion on their own.

Typically, I script three to five initiating questions for each piece of text to be used in a Socratic circle. Before the activity begins, I select one of the questions to be used with the first inner circle, but I never pick the second inner circle's initiating question until after I have heard the dialogue of the first circle. In this way, my initiating question for the second inner circle can help to refocus or maybe even redirect the group to an area the first group missed or glossed over. And sometimes, I compose an entirely new initiating question for the second circle as the first circle is engaged in dialogue. Having three to five initiating questions scripted in advance allows a teacher to be flexible and responsive to the dialogue's direction and flow.

Once the initiating question has been posed and students have begun creating their dialogue, it is time for the teacher to begin allowing the students to take the reins of the discussion. Of course, the teacher is still nearby to take those reins back if the horses begin to run wild and out of control, but he or she should take on much more of an observer or facilitator role in the conversation.

By far the most labor-intensive aspect of leading a Socratic circle is facilitating the inner circle's conversation, guiding and coaching students through the process without dictating the topic and direction of their discussion. Certainly, a balance must be reached between the teacher participating too much and not participating enough. Often, this balance determines the success of the Socratic circle itself. Teachers must call forth their "inner Socrates"—and help students do the same—to do this effectively. By helping students adequately prepare for dialogue, showing them methods of annotating text, offering a high-quality initiating question, and then manipulating the dynamics of the group, a teacher can greatly influence the overall quality of the classroom dialogue.

WHAT IF STUDENTS WON'T TALK?

One of the most frequently asked questions about Socratic circles is what the teacher should do if no one in the inner circle will talk. Fortunately, this almost never happens. Students love to talk and love to share their opinions. This activity taps into this interest and channels it into a productive and meaningful classroom experience. The fear of students not talking or even of not having enough to say to fill the allotted time rarely materializes. If it does, it is more than likely because of one of three reasons: (1) the topic the text addresses makes students uncomfortable in discussion with their peers or in the presence of an adult, (2) students cannot identify or make connections with the text that allow them to explore the underlying philosophical questions the text seeks to address, or (3) students found the text too difficult or did not spend enough time preparing for the dialogue. If one of these three situations arises, there are steps that a teacher can take to alleviate the concern and stimulate the dialogue that needs to occur.

If students appear uncomfortable with the issues brought about by the text, a leader can ask them to explore their comfort level as part of the opening question. "I'm sensing that some of you are feeling uncomfortable with the ideas expressed in this text. What is it about these issues that makes you uncomfortable?" Often student dialogue about their reactions to the text eases the transition into a more philosophical exploration of the ideas contained within. Another method of handling student discomfort is by modeling for students your own reactions and feelings about the text. "I can be totally honest in telling you all that some of the issues brought up here leave me feeling a bit uncomfortable. I'm hoping that through our dialogue we all will have a better understanding of the issues involved and the reasons we have for feeling awkward about them." Ultimately, Socratic circles are based on the idea that classrooms are centers for communities of learning. Students must feel that teachers are willing participants who approach the Socratic circle process with the same questions, interests, and devotion that they themselves are being asked to share. Showing students our own apprehension is often enough to increase their comfort and stimulate dialogue.

Like feeling comfortable, the connections that students make to their own lives and their own experiences are crucial for good dialogue. Students are reluctant to discuss an idea or an issue that seemingly has no relevance to their lives. Helping students make connections to the text often activates prior knowledge and provides a foundation upon which this new learning and thinking can be placed. Again, effective opening questions can greatly increase the connections students make with a piece of text. Simple questions such as, When you first read this text, what kinds of things did it remind you of? Or, Has anyone been through a situation similar to what is being described in this text? can help students identify these connections and begin dialogue. The Socratic circle leader modeling a connection to his or her own life can also be an effective way to cultivate connections. "Every time I read this piece, I think about the movie The *Shawshank Redemption* and the message of the importance of hope that is conveyed at the end. Can anyone else explain this connection?" Beginning with a connection of one's own can encourage the connections of others and lead to more fruitful dialogue for all those involved.

Finally, when students appear unprepared for dialogue or complain that the text is too difficult, the leader can temporarily take a more participatory role and guide the inner circle through the text until the students can take over. Using Socratic questioning here again addresses this situation. "Let's take a look at the first sentence in this piece of text. Why do you think the author chose to begin with such a disturbing and vivid image?" Or "Can anyone say in a sentence or two the main idea of this passage?" Questioning such as this might continue until students begin devising their own lines of questioning and their own topics for discussion. When this occurs, the leader can simply pull back out of the more participatory role and allow the dialogue to continue on its own.

Again, students will talk and share their opinions and insights into a selection of text just as they will in any discussion. In all my experience with Socratic circles, I have never had a circle not talk. At times, there is initial resistance to the topic or to the issues involved. But with open-ended, low-risk questioning, students can be motivated and encouraged to share, and dialogue will ensue.

BREAKING THE HABITS OF TRADITIONAL DISCUSSION

Another issue in facilitating the inner circle involves helping students adjust to the idea of dialogue after years of experience with more traditional styles of classroom discussion. In my classes, the early part of the school year is when students need the most urging to engage in this new form of conversation. If they are reluctant to take the reins of the conversation and depend upon me to ask follow-up questions or stimulate new areas of discussion, I oblige them. In some classes, I have even left the neutral confines of the teacher's role and sat with the inner circle, participating just as the students do, offering opinions, asking questions, and sometimes feigning ignorance to force the group into deeper conversation on their own. By sitting and participating with the inner circle, I serve a twofold purpose. It models the kind of behavior I am looking for in the inner circle and provides an opportunity to verbally praise the students who take that initial leap and begin to guide the conversations themselves. This hands-on coaching begins to break down the barriers of the teacher-student roles in traditional class discussions and reinforces for students the goals and behaviors I am looking for in their dialogue.

Another successful strategy to help students begin to guide and control the conversation on their own can be implemented within the feedback discussion of the outer circle. After the first time around the outer circle to hear students' initial observations and comments, I sometimes ask very direct, very specific questions designed to help students in both the inner and outer circles better understand the purpose and importance of the inner circle's dialogue. For example, I might pose a question such as, When I asked the question about the double meaning in the seventh line of the poem, what did you notice about where possible answers to my question were directed? Students in the outer circle can quickly identify that the inner circle's answers were not directed to the circle itself, but to me specifically. We then emphasize that we must be mindful about directing our ideas to the group as a whole rather than to the individual who posed the question. In future Socratic circles, if I notice a similar problem, a simple circular hand gesture over the heads of the inner circle is often enough to remind students to direct their responses to the entire group rather than one individual. This reduces my involvement in the conversation and leaves the guidance of the conversation's direction in the students' hands. Coaching such as this can be very effective in helping students adapt to the different focus of student-centered dialogue.

A final strategy I use in making this adjustment is simple silence. Although I would never use this technique early in the year when students are still learning the process of participating in the activity, it can be effective with classes that have completed a handful of Socratic circles and have some degree of experience under their belts. There seems to be a point after four or five Socratic circles when students erroneously believe they have the Socratic circle concept all figured out. In my classes we talk about this period and I use the analogy of bicycle training wheels. Once students have learned the process and think they have mastered it, there comes a point where the teacher cannot catch them if they begin to fall; the training wheels must be removed and they must proceed on two wheels rather than four. My silence is often their first exposure to this principle, and, although uncomfortable at first, most classes adapt fairly quickly. When used at the right time, this "sink or swim" mentality is very effective in pushing students to greater heights of dialogue.

KNOWING WHAT QUESTIONS TO ASK

Because classroom dialogue is relatively open-ended and can progress down a plethora of avenues, some teachers struggle to decide which questions are appropriate and which are not appropriate to ask the inner circle. Asking the right types of questions can be critical to Socratic circle success. However, there is no blueprint for what specific questions to ask or even when they should be asked. Generally, questions should be open-ended, philosophical in nature, and help participants explore the meaning and importance of the issues raised in the text. Questions for a Socratic circle fall into one of two categories: those we script out before the dialogue begins and those we generate as the dialogue is progressing.

I typically sit down the night before a Socratic circle and script out ten to fifteen potential questions that I might use during the next day's conversation. Of course, it may be that students launch into dialogue without the need for my input and my questions are never used, or their discussion may take them in a direction that is completely different from my line of questioning. Regardless, I prefer to have a few questions ready in case the circles struggle with finding material to discuss. I would much rather have questions that are never posed than have students never fully engage with a piece of text.

In *A Guide for Leaders of Great Books Discussion Groups*, Mortimer Adler proposes that there are three types of questions: fact, interpretation, and evaluation: "What does the author say? What does the author mean? Is it true?" As I prepare my questions for a Socratic circle, I try to include a few from each category.

In other words, some of my questions ask students to refer to the text and find examples or particular information. ("Contrasts and opposites play a large role in this poem. Can you find examples?") These low-risk questions have specific answers and often rely more on memory than thinking. They typically serve to focus student attention on a particular element of the text and are often followed with another question that requires students to do something with the factual information they have just identified.

Some of my questions—the interpretive—then ask students to describe what the author is trying to convey. ("What does this author really mean when she says, 'I've heard that before, but not from anyone I cared about'?") These questions have multiple answers that students can agree or disagree with and then explain to the group the reasons for their opinions.

The last type of questions—the evaluative—asks the students to step outside the text and consider the implications of what is being described. ("How would you personally handle a situation similar to the one being described by this author?") These questions, too, are open-ended and intended to solicit personal opinions that the group can use as a spring-board for further discussion. Therefore, these evaluative questions are sometimes very general in nature. ("How is this concept important in our own lives?" or "Why is this idea something we should care about?")

Typically, an evaluative question is not asked without a line of lower-risk questions coming before it.

No amount of planning, and no number of prewritten questions, however, will fully prepare a leader for an individual dialogue. Students will bring their own ideas, their own opinions, and their own experiences to the discussion that will greatly influence the flow and direction of the conversation. A teacher must be able to think "on the fly" and generate new questions that will tap the reserves of what is being discussed and guide students to deeper and more fruitful levels of dialogue. With practice, teachers begin thinking of new questions of each of these three types continuously throughout the dialogue, and when a question is posed to the inner circle, students have no way of knowing if it was spontaneously generated or scripted the night before.

ENCOURAGING MORE MEANINGFUL DIALOGUE

Once dialogue has been established and students have begun to feel comfortable with the praxis of Socratic circles, teachers can begin to exert more guidance of the dialogue's content. However, teachers must be attentive to maintaining the balance between not participating in the conversation enough and participating too much, dictating its direction and flow. With time teachers begin to gain a feel for when and how they can and should contribute to student dialogue and guide it toward deeper, higher-level thinking and conversation.

The primary way to help students explore the content of the text more thoroughly and deeply is through Socratic questioning. As explained above, generating a list of potential questions before the Socratic circle (much as one would for a more traditional classroom discussion) can be very effective. Where teachers need to focus their attention is on finding the proper place to insert those questions into the discussion. A well-placed teacher question can stimulate great dialogue; a poorly placed teacher question can stymie dialogue and leave students feeling misinformed, underappreciated, and overly controlled. Teachers should keep in mind when generating potential questions that not all questions will be used in a particular Socratic circle and that those used with a class early in the day might be completely different from those used with a class later in the day.

Paying close attention to the direction and content of student dialogue is important to understanding when and how to interrupt the conversation's natural flow. In my experience leading Socratic circles over the last several years, I have noticed that students tend to focus too intently on specific, tangible details of the text without generalizing the ideas being presented and embracing multiple perspectives on those details.

Absorbing the dialogue and using the ideas and references students generate to help them back away from the details they are discussing can be particularly helpful in raising their dialogue to the next level.

One of the ways I help students do this is by suggesting they contemplate a situation similar to the one being described in the text that shares some of the underlying characteristics and realities. Often this occurs in the form of a visualization exercise, beginning with the phrase "Imagine you were . . . ." Once students have discussed the problematic similar situation, I might follow up with a question such as, How do you think this author [or this speaker] might react if facing this situation? Encouraging students to explore how different individuals might solve problems or react to certain situations often helps them consider the more general implications and ultimately helps them create dialogue that is more insightful and philosophical.

Another method of helping students probe more deeply with their dialogue comes from helping them draw connections and recognize similarities among various interpretations they might be considering. With practice in Socratic circles, students become very adept at embracing multiple perspectives and interpretations of text but often struggle in drawing conclusions from comparing those perspectives. Quickly summarizing the perspectives offered and asking students to discuss the similarities they see among them generates new thinking and discussion about the text. Then, after students have identified those similarities, asking them to verbalize the generalized principles those similarities embody often broadens and deepens their dialogue.

By far the most effective way to foster deeper, more philosophical dialogue is to praise students for their insights and encourage them to praise their peers. This can be done not only in the context of the Socratic circle but in the activities that follow it as well. Seeing profound ideas developed through dialogue appear in a piece of student writing is a wonderful opportunity for such praise. Ultimately, when students begin to realize that the dialogue they are creating is providing them with insight that is shaping their learning and improving their grades, they are intrinsically motivated to elevate their dialogue to higher and higher levels of critical thought and discussion.

Unfortunately, there is no single, clear answer or methodology for how teachers should facilitate more philosophical student dialogue. Each selection of text, each group of students, and the variables of time, setting, and context all exert profound influence over the direction and flow of the conversation. Teacher preparation, flexibility, open-mindedness, and creativity are keys to helping guide students to unlock the mysteries of insight and epiphany. Ultimately, we can provide them the keys, but the deadbolts must be turned by their own hands.

MANAGING THE DYNAMICS OF THE INNER CIRCLE

Once the process of Socratic circles is established and the teacher begins to feel comfortable with the conversation taking place within the inner circle, we can begin to manipulate the dynamics of the group to create more effective and higher-quality dialogue. Students bent on distracting the group, students who monopolize the conversation, students with rude or inappropriate comments lacking common courtesy, and conflicts that develop between and among students can all adversely affect the Socratic circle. Dealing with these obstacles and, more important, coaching students to overcome them is an important component of facilitating the inner circle.

Handling Students Who Distract the Group

As with all learning situations, classroom management is an important component of creating an environment in which all students can grow and develop. Socratic circles are no different. And although Socratic circles do reduce classroom disruptions and help instill in students a more cooperative attitude, there are occasions when individual behavior works against the collective good of the group and against the strategy itself. Perhaps most disruptive and frustrating is the student who feels the need to distract either the inner circle or the outer circle from their goals and objectives.

Our jobs as teachers and our classroom roles as instructional leaders demand that we counteract such disruption. Within a Socratic circle, this can seem on the surface to be more difficult than it is in other learning situations. Because the teacher is doing his or her best to allow the dialogue to develop with as little influence or guidance as possible, it can be difficult to manage such situations. Action needs to be taken to refocus the class and continue with the activity, but such action must also be done with as little disruption and interference as possible. There are a number of strategies for dealing with just such a situation.

One of the easiest and least interruptive methods of addressing the behavior of a disruptive student is with a simple one-word verbal command. I often use the word "focus" to bring the disruption to a halt and recenter the group on the task at hand. This strategy can be used for a multitude of disruptions, from students who attempt to guide the dialogue down a path of absurdity, to students who are overly critical of others' ideas, to students with annoying habits that draw attention from the ideas being considered. The verbal command serves as a quick and painless reminder of the purpose of the student conversation, and often-times can refocus multiple students who may not be devoting their full attention to the dialogue. Students will rarely be able to identify the specific misbehavior that prompted the teacher's comment, but will quickly take stock of their own behavior, wondering if they are the source.

A more demonstrative way to refocus the group's attention is by interjecting a question into the inner circle's conversation. This is particularly useful when the verbal cue "focus" has been used but has not been entirely effective. Posing a new question or a question that serves to refocus the conversation of the inner circle restarts the dialogue in many ways. It allows all students a moment to metaphorically catch their breath, consider the question, and reengage with the group. This also serves as a cue to the misbehaving student that the teacher is listening to the conversation and will not allow the dialogue to drift too far from the topic or waste too much time spinning its wheels.

For behaviors that may distract the group for only a few seconds or draw only partial attention away from the conversation, I typically wait until I am directing the discussion of the outer circle before addressing the situation, especially early in the school year. Because much of the teacher's role within a Socratic circle is that of coaching students through the process, at times it is effective to allow students to wallow in their minor mistakes. By directing attention to the misbehavior during the outer circle's discussion, students are able to predict how the dialogue might have been different had the misbehavior not occurred. This is particularly effective in helping students create their own methods of dealing with such occurrences and allows them the opportunity to establish goals to correct such problems in the future. After witnessing and addressing such disruptive behavior once, students are quick to identify similar behaviors on the part of others and point them out to the class as a whole. Oftentimes, constructive criticism from peers is far more effective in changing student behavior than teacher criticism is.

For disruptions that are more severe in nature—offensive language, personal verbal attacks, obstinate refusal to engage in the conversation—I prefer to remove the student from the activity. Depending on the severity of the offense and on the personality of the particular student, I have the student sit in a chair, sometimes beside me, sometimes in the far corner of the room, sometimes in the hallway with the door propped open so that the student can hear the conversation but cannot participate. Because Socratic circles create student ownership over the material and the process, many students view being removed from them as a fate worse than death. Forcing them to observe without allowing them to participate is an unsatisfying consequence. And many times after class, I have heard one student chastise another one for being removed from the dialogue, because students know that every voice is important and that silencing individual voices ultimately harms the overall quality of the ideas that are generated.

For severe misbehavior and disruption of the learning activity, I also follow up with consequences prescribed by both my classroom management plan and my building discipline plan. But regardless of the severity of such misbehavior, occurrences such as these are also learning opportunities for students that can prompt social growth and goal setting for future Socratic circles. The cooperative nature and collaborative quality of the dialogue process is such that student misbehaviors and disruptions are by far the exception rather than the rule.

Handling Students Who Monopolize the Conversation

Like the student who distracts the group from dialogue, the student who behaves in the opposite manner—monopolizing the conversation within the inner circle—is just as difficult. Often a student will be so engaged and so interested in a particular topic or text that he or she, sometimes without conscious knowledge, dominates the discussion and other students have trouble voicing their ideas and opinions. As a teacher, this can be difficult to manage without damaging the ego of the over-zealous students and potentially damaging the climate that is crucial to Socratic circle success.

Ideally, other students within the inner circle will handle this situation. Dialogue experience teaches students that all opinions and ideas have value and could possibly lead the group to higher and greater understanding. Many students will be able to encourage a peer who is dominating the conversation to allow other voices into the mix for the benefit of the group. Most students understand that the needs of the group outweigh their individual needs to be heard and understood. However, when a student struggles to understand this concept, or when students are not yet experienced and comfortable enough with the Socratic circle process to suggest it, it is the teacher's job to step in and mediate a resolution.

There are many ways to accomplish this, depending on the severity of the student's domination. Often within the context of a particular Socratic circle one student will be emotionally attached to a particular idea, concept, or position and determined to defend it seemingly until his or her last breath. Sometimes this is helping the group explore meaning, but other times it impedes the group from moving forward and examining other ideas. Here, the leader stepping in and redirecting the dialogue with another open-ended question, one that skirts the concept so strongly embraced by the controlling student, best diffuses the situation. Some students may be so involved that it takes multiple interruptions on the part of the leader with new questions to refocus the group.

Occasionally, a student will be of the mind-set that Socratic circles are his or her opportunity to indoctrinate other students into his or her own philosophy. When this occurs, the student will tend to try to dominate many or all Socratic circles, regardless of the text or content. Talking with the student privately outside of class and encouraging him or her to allow other ideas and points of view in the dialogue is the best way to handle this situation. Teachers might even want to place a specific value on the number of times an individual student contributes to a Socratic circle. "Johnny, I really appreciate your eagerness and your willingness to participate. But in order to encourage others to be more open with their ideas, I would appreciate it if you would hold yourself to five contributions per discussion." This still allows the student to speak and actually encourages higher-level thinking, because he or she must evaluate ahead of time which comments to make before the group. When this is done privately, other students in the class are not even aware of the limitations being placed on this student.

Finally, there have been times that I have had large numbers of very eager, very engaged students in the same class who almost completely squelch the voices of others in Socratic circles. In this situation, I have found it most helpful to use an ante system for student contributions to the dialogue. Using poker chips, tongue depressors from the nurse's office, or leftover pencils from standardized testing, I dole out a given number of tokens to each student (three seems to work best with a ten-minute conversation). Each time a student contributes, he or she must "ante up." When a student runs out of tokens, he or she must wait until all students are out of tokens before making another comment. This helps to ensure that at least the beginning of the dialogue is balanced with a diversity of student opinions and voices. I have also used this strategy with classes that have not had problems with overly dominating students. Almost unanimously, the students hate the system. They think it is too obtrusive, and detrimental to a fruitful dialogue. In most cases, the simple threat of pulling out the poker chips is enough to make students take stock of the frequency and length of participation.

Managing Disagreements Among Students

Another fear of almost all teachers when they first consider employing Socratic circles (myself included) is of a verbal or physical argument erupting between students. Fortunately, this very rarely happens. Like many teachers I feared the possibilities in turning over so much control to my students, especially when I knew they would be openly discussing their ideas and opinions, sometimes on emotionally charged topics. I imagined shouting matches, machismo posturing, emotional outbursts and the subsequent hurt feelings, damaged egos, and shaken senses of moral reality. Fortunately, my experience with Socratic circles has been much, much different.

I am continually amazed at how mature students can act when given the opportunity to do so. Although there have been exceptions, the vast majority of my Socratic circles have been calm, positive, and supportive discussions even when there was strong disagreement among the participants. When exceptions do occur, the teacher must act quickly and decisively to restore order. Most times simply halting the conversation and asking for a moment of silence for everyone to catch their breath and reflect is a starting point. Following this with a simple question such as, The purpose of a Socratic circle is to create a collective understanding of a piece of text or an issue. Is what just happened helping us meet our goal? will often end the disruption. Most students will disrupt the flow of a Socratic circle only when they are overcome with emotion. Simply asking them to take a moment to step back from the situation and look at it from a more objective point of view is sufficient in most circumstances. In my classroom, I have never had an outburst proceed past that point.

The possibility—however unlikely—for further problems is there, and the teacher should be prepared for them. Temporarily removing a student or students from the inner circle is a recommended consequence for misbehavior. Students look forward to Socratic circles, and the idea of being excluded from participating in one is a reality most would not want to face. Following up with one-on-one conferences to discuss the reasons that led to the misbehavior is also strongly suggested. In this way teachers can better identify the antecedents of misbehavior and reduce the likelihood of such events happening in the future.

CONCLUSION

Facilitating the inner circle and finding ways to help the members approach the text and one another greatly improves their dialogue and the conversation skills of the entire class. By helping students to prepare for, initiate, and manage the dialogue they create in class, we can teach lifelong skills that will serve them throughout their lives. Coaching and guiding the inner circle with praise, modeling, and the Socratic method are all important components of this process. Allowing students to take ownership of their inquiry, thereby creating choice and developing their voices, can be a powerful addition to classroom learning.

Chapter 5

FACILITATING THE OUTER CIRCLE

SAMPLE OUTER CIRCLE CONVERSATION.

AARON: *Overall I was really impressed with what the inner circle came up with, but there was a lot of interrupting going on and some bickering back and forth between a couple of people. And I know that disagreement is good and all and that it helps to move the conversation forward and explore new ideas, but I think it could have been handled better. In a couple of spots you guys were downright rude.*

COPELAND: *That's a good observation, Aaron, and an idea I was hoping someone would bring up. What were your initial observations, Sam?*

SAMANTHA: *I kind of agree with Aaron. Your ideas were really good, but sometimes I think a couple of people in the group were more concerned with others thinking they were right than they were with helping the group move forward. Sometimes it seems like we get bogged down with one or two people arguing over something and the whole conversation just kind of stops and doesn't go anywhere.*

COPELAND: *Excellent point. We lost track of goal there for a while, didn't we? Patrick, your thoughts?*

PATRICK: *I agree that the conversation wasn't as civil and polite as it could have been, but I disagree with what Samantha said. I do think that the disagreement helped move the*

75

conversation forward. If it hadn't been for the arguing over whether or not the man was holding a knife in the painting, the group might not have ever explored how the fight scene in the foreground affected the entire mood of the painting.

COPELAND: *Good, I'm glad you pointed that out, Patrick. That's an excellent point to keep in mind. How about you Ashley, what did you see?*

ASHLEY: *I agree with all of you. The disagreement and arguing helped to figure things out, but I still think you could have found a better way to approach your disagreement. Socratic circles aren't supposed to be competitions; they're supposed to be conversations. What bothered me more was that no one else in the circle tried to calm down the argument between Josh and Aaron. Everybody was just content to sit back and watch the fireworks. I'd like to see the group be more responsible as a whole and keep each other moving forward.*

As one can see from the conversation above, the outer circle's role of providing feedback on the inner circle's behavior is crucial to the improvement of students' discussion skills. Many students take the comments of their peers much more to heart than they do the comments of a teacher. And the knowledge that the outer circle will be evaluated in the same manner as the inner circle later in the class period helps to keep the feedback constructive and more positive in nature.

The teacher's role in the Socratic circle process changes dramatically as the students shift their attention from the dialogue of the inner circle to the feedback of the outer circle. Whereas in the inner circle the teacher is guiding or coaching students through their dialogue, he or she takes on a far more participatory role in the outer circle and directs the student conversation, seeking answers and solutions to improving the quality of the dialogue for the future.

The outer circle's observations, critiques, and suggestions are crucial to the improvement of the conversation in the inner circle. It is the outer circle that provides feedback to guide participants through the process of improvement. Teachers can take steps to help students prepare to discuss the dialogue of the inner circle by using the steps of critical reflection (reflective thinking, self-assessment, and goal setting) and can help students monitor their own contributions, balancing praise and constructive criticism. Effectively using Socratic questioning can also help to maintain the students' sense of ownership and empowerment within the conversation of the outer circle as they wait their turn to engage in the dialogue of the inner circle.

PREPARING FOR THE DISCUSSION OF THE OUTER CIRCLE

Preparing for the discussion of the outer circle is just as important as preparing for the dialogue of the inner circle. However, because the outer circle's task is centered on responding to the performance of the inner circle, preparation takes a much different form. Although the discussion of the outer circle is much more teacher centered than the dialogue of the inner circle, student ownership of the content of the conversation can be maintained with the use of critical reflection and Socratic questioning.

Critical Reflection

To think critically and responsively about the dialogue that occurs within the inner circle, I lead a discussion of the outer circle that follows the elements of critical reflection (Copeland and Grout 2004). Rather than focusing on the content of the inner circle's dialogue, the outer circle focuses on the inner circle's behavior and process, reflecting on their experiences, assessing the quality of their dialogue, and establishing goals for future performance. By following a simple pattern during this conversation, we are able to offer constructive feedback that, over time, greatly enhances our Socratic circles.

Critical reflection is a cyclical process. It begins with a learning experience and then moves to three distinct stages of reflection: reflective thinking, self-assessment, and goal setting. The praxis of dialogue and reflection spurs growth as problems from one dialogue are identified during reflection and improvements are made during subsequent dialogues. Freire (1993) envisions this process of action, reflection, further action, and further reflection as an upward spiral, climbing and improving as behaviors and skills are constantly reexamined.

In a Socratic circle, the dialogue of the inner circle provides the learning experience, and the outer circle's discussion moves the class through the stages of reflection, self-assessment, and goal setting. Ideally, the four steps flow together so smoothly that they appear basically seamless.

The initial step of the reflection process of the outer circle is reflective thinking. Simply put, reflective thinking is thinking about what you have already done. However, reflective thinking is far more complex than many people realize. Reflective thinking is closely linked to critical thinking, because as people move through the steps of the reflective thinking process, they begin to question, assess, organize, reason, hypothesize, and predict. At the heart of reflective thinking is the questioning of skills, perspectives, and behaviors that make up performance. And this questioning is both the basis for and the result of reflective thinking.

These questions then help the outer circle begin to assess the performance of the inner circle. In my classes this is done by rating the performance of the inner circle on a simple scale of one to ten. This provides immediate feedback for the inner circle and helps the entire class put their performance in a particular dialogue in a context with other dialogues. Students can begin to make mental comparisons and value judgments on their own performance and the performance of their group.

The natural result of this reflective thinking and self-assessment is the establishment of goals for future learning. To establish goals and thus improve learning, students must be able to accurately determine where they stand in the process, what skills and materials they have already acquired, and what skills and materials they still need. Students are often very adept at creating their own goals for their learning. One of the benefits of goal setting and critical reflection is that by thinking about their own behavior, thinking, and working, students are able to identify areas for improvement and growth. Critical reflection allows students to become experts and guides of their own education. Establishing goals in Socratic circles allows students to control and manipulate their own behavior and learning. In this manner, students learn to become the self-directed, holistic learners the public seeks to create.

The necessity of goal setting in the critical reflection process cannot be underestimated. The thorough and effective establishment of goals provides the link from the dialogue of one inner circle to another and from one Socratic circle to another. Goal setting is essential for the cycle of critical reflection to take hold and provide students with meaningful growth and learning. By focusing the discussion of the outer circle on these three stages, the feedback we offer the inner circle is more complete and fruitful in moving the quality of our dialogue forward.

Feedback Form

To prepare my students for reflective thinking and their discussion of what they witness in the conversation of the inner circle, I usually share Figure 5.1 with them for the first few Socratic circles of the school year. Having students work with this form helps to focus their attention, and I make suggestions about the behaviors they should be paying attention to as they observe the dialogue of the inner circle. After our first few Socratic circles, students no longer need the feedback form and can respond critically and insightfully without it.

This feedback form, with its combination of close-ended and open-ended questions, asks students to identify and rate the behaviors of the group as a whole and its individual members. Focusing on such behaviors as speaking loudly and clearly, avoiding hostile exchanges, using the text

FIGURE 5.1
Feedback Form

Socratic Circle Feedback Form

Name _____ Hour_____ Date_____

1. Rate the inner circle's performance on the following criteria: (circle the appropriate number)

Did the participants . . .	Poor		Average		Excellent
dig below the surface meaning?	1	2	3	4	5
speak loudly and clearly?	1	2	3	4	5
cite reasons and evidence for their statements?	1	2	3	4	5
use the text to find support?	1	2	3	4	5
listen to others respectfully?	1	2	3	4	5
stick with the subject?	1	2	3	4	5
talk to each other, not just the leader?	1	2	3	4	5
paraphrase accurately?	1	2	3	4	5
avoid inappropriate language?	1	2	3	4	5
ask for help to clear up confusion?	1	2	3	4	5
support each other?	1	2	3	4	5
avoid hostile exchanges?	1	2	3	4	5
question others in a civil manner?	1	2	3	4	5
seem prepared?	1	2	3	4	5
make sure questions were understood?	1	2	3	4	5

2. Name specific people who did one or more of the above criteria well.

3. What was the most interesting question asked?

4. What was the most interesting idea to come from a participant?

5. What was the best thing you observed?

6. What was the most troubling thing you observed?

7. How could this troubling thing be corrected or improved?

to support ideas, and asking for help in clearing up moments of confusion helps the group examine the skills that are necessary for high-quality conversation and dialogue to occur. The open-ended questions toward the bottom of the form then ask observers to identify specific individuals who demonstrate these behaviors. This allows students in the outer circle to note specific items that can then be mentioned in the outer circle's discussion. Like the annotations of text students make for the inner circle, these notes serve as a warehouse of ideas that can be drawn upon in discussion.

Typically I spend very little time teaching the procedures of the feedback form; I prefer to use the discussion of the outer circle itself as an opportunity to praise and reinforce students who make insightful comments about the dialogue and who use the form to help them think more deeply and critically about the conversation they have witnessed. Although I spend little time teaching the form itself, we do spend a few minutes the first day discussing the importance of honest and constructive feedback that focuses on the behaviors of individuals and not on the individuals themselves. I also reinforce that the purpose of the feedback form is to help the class as a whole improve our discussion skills and examine our performance more closely; it is not an opportunity to point out faults, pass judgment or blame, or criticize others unjustly.

Early in the Socratic circle process, the feedback form serves my classes well as an effective method of centering student attention on useful discussion. However, some students respond unfavorably to the feedback form for a variety of reasons. Some are uncomfortable at first with the idea of pointing out flaws in the conversation behaviors of their peers. Whether they fear retribution or feel guilty for being critical, these students typically write few comments on the feedback form, and the comments they do make may be very superficial. Focusing the nature of the outer-circle discussion on being supportive and helpful eases this problem and helps students in the outer circle expand the number and depth of their comments. For classes that seem to have a particularly difficult time adapting to the need for effective feedback, I sometimes assign points to the completion of the form and the quality of feedback offered to reinforce the practice. Generally, this needs to be done only once or twice to convey the feedback form's importance.

After students have completed their first few Socratic circles, the outer circle's conversation progresses nicely without the use of the feedback form. There comes a point at which students become more concerned with filling out the form than with consciously observing the dialogue of the inner circle. When I see this happening, I generally abandon the feedback form and instead have students note their observations on the back of the selection of text. This allows them to have ideas to reference in their discussion while also allowing them to devote more of their attention to the dialogue itself. Many students find the form too restrictive after multiple uses and prefer to note their observations in a more open-ended fashion.

STARTING THE PROCESS OF OUTER-CIRCLE DISCUSSION

To explain the role of the outer circle on the day of our first Socratic circle, I activate prior knowledge and ask students to think of the police dramas they have watched on television and in movies. Specifically we discuss those scenes in which a witness or an alleged criminal is seated in an interrogation room to be interviewed by detectives. In those interrogation rooms is typically a one-way mirror that allows people to observe and listen to the conversation without allowing the witness or alleged criminal to be aware that he or she is being observed. Students are familiar with these scenes and can usually think of many shows and movies in which this occurs.

I then explain to students that their role in the outer circle is similar to the role of the detectives or lawyers standing behind those one-way mirrors—their job is to watch and listen in such a manner that their presence is never detected. Using this model often helps students understand their role in the outer circle, but I also explain that what they are watching and listening for is very different than those people watching a police interrogation. Rather than focusing their attention on *what* is being said, students in the outer circle should focus on the human behavior of *how* those ideas are presented. Students should look for such things as who speaks the most, who speaks the least, who asks the best questions, who offers the most insightful answers, who leads the group, who distracts the group from achieving their goals, and so on.

This short set of instructions, coupled with the basic explanation of the feedback form, suffices to explain the duties of the outer circle in a Socratic circle. At this point, the inner circle begins their conversation focused on the text and students in the outer circle quietly observe.

Offering Initial Observations and Feedback

For the duration of the inner circle's conversation, the outer circle is noting their observations and preparing to offer the inner circle feedback as soon as they have finished. To begin this feedback session, I have students go around the outer circle and offer their initial comments and observations. In terms of the process of critical reflection, this stage represents reflective thinking. Students in the outer circle are deliberating and weighing the effectiveness and appropriateness of the behaviors of the members of the inner circle, all while the inner circle students listen silently.

The outer circle's comments and observations are always some of the most interesting moments of a Socratic circle, for their insight and for their eagerness to spur improvement. Progressing around the outer circle means each student is held accountable for observing and preparing feedback for the inner circle. And although some feedback is repetitive, even the repetition is useful to the inner circle. Oftentimes hearing the same comment repeated by several students helps the inner circle honestly consider the point and think more seriously about ways to improve that area.

This internal questioning on the part of the inner circle—questioning that is generated by the feedback of the outer circle—is particularly effective in producing growth and improvement over time. Generally, I keep my comments and opinions about the inner circle's performance to a bare minimum, commenting only to elaborate upon a point mentioned by a student or to highlight an issue missed by the outer circle. The majority of my contributions to the outer circle's discussion are in the form of questions. Generating questions of my own to guide the discussion in the outer circle benefits students in both circles. And although the outer circle wasn't involved directly in the dialogue of the inner circle, they learn vicariously through the experiences they have witnessed.

After we have journeyed around the outer circle hearing students' initial comments and suggestions, I lead the outer circle in a closer examination of some of their feedback. Typically, as I observe the dialogue of the inner circle, I am jotting notes about their performance just as the students in the outer circle are. Using those notes as a sort of checklist, I proceed with a line of Socratic questioning for the outer circle on what they witnessed in the performance of the inner circle. For example, if I notice a particularly strong moment of leadership on the part of one of the students in the inner circle, I might examine that moment more closely with the outer circle. I might start by asking, "What examples of leadership did you see in this conversation?" Students might then generate several student names from the inner circle and several examples of leadership for discussion. Eventually, whether on their own accord or with me asking, What other examples of leadership did you see?, students will identify the specific moment that I want to discuss. Once students have pinpointed the student I want to discuss, I continue with the line of Socratic questioning: How did Suzy show leadership? What was particularly effective in Suzy using this method? How might we be able to use this idea in our own inner circles of the future?

In this manner I can direct the feedback of the outer circle, covering all the points noted about the inner circle's dialogue—but by my asking questions, the feedback the inner circle hears comes from other students rather than from me. This is an important point. Students often take the comments and constructive criticism of their fellow students much more seriously and much more to heart than they do the comments and the criticism of the teacher. Hearing their peers offer ideas, opinions, and suggestions on how the inner circle can improve empowers those students to make improvements happen. If I as a teacher make the same suggestions, students feel as though they are being judged and graded on their performance. But to hear those comments from peers removes the stigma of being graded by a teacher. They certainly are still being judged, but the assessment is less formal in their minds and far more constructive in helping them improve.

Using a line of Socratic questioning as I lead the discussion of the outer circle greatly assists me in helping my students see the value of classroom discussion and stimulating a desire for constant improvement. Students feel a sense of accomplishment with their inner-circle dialogue when it goes well and insightful meaning is constructed. Students learn quickly that the feedback offered by the outer circle, although not always easy to hear and assimilate, can be of great assistance in improving their dialogue and achieving those moments of epiphany on a more consistent basis.

Self-Assessment

After hearing the initial comments from students and after exploring a line of Socratic questioning to cover my notes on the inner circle's dialogue, I ask the outer circle to rate the quality of the inner circle's performance on a scale of one to ten. Sometimes I ask specific students in the outer circle to do this, and sometimes I ask for a more general response from the circle as a whole. In either case, I seek to hear ratings from several different students, on occasion asking them to give a one-sentence explanation of their rating. Surprisingly the ratings usually are within a point or so of each other and, more often than not, are in line with the rating I would give the inner circle as well. After just a few Socratic circles, students grasp the concept and are quite accurate in their ratings. For those occasions when as a class we hear a rating significantly different from the others, we ask that student to explain his or her reasons for the rating, focusing on both the strengths of the inner circle and the areas thought to need improvement.

These ratings serve several important purposes. First, they give the inner circle immediate feedback on the overall quality of their dialogue. Although the feedback and observations are far more important in terms of their growth and development with the process, the numeric rating gives them an assessment of that day's performance. And although I strive to have my students focus on the process and the idea of continuous improvement, the outer circle's rating is as important to them as the feedback itself. Over time, however, those ratings help them track their performance and growth. By comparing the numeric rating of one Socratic circle with previous Socratic circles, students have a sense of whether or not they are improving, and coupled with the feedback received from the outer circle, can determine whether they have achieved the goals they outlined from the previous Socratic circle.

For some students, the self-assessment rating offers another important opportunity, and although this is not the purpose of engaging in Socratic circles, some find the competition between the two inner circles motivating. The rating given to the first inner circle provides the students in the second inner circle with a clear and specific target, and for some students the thrill of competition is a secondary factor that motivates their performance. And although this competition appears to pit one group of students against another, the real competition is among the students of the second inner circle as to whether or not they apply the feedback they gave to the first inner circle to their own dialogue.

Goal Setting

Before switching circles, the final step in the critical reflection process and the one most important in continuous improvement is goal setting. After the outer circle has reflected on the performance of the inner circle and offered both feedback and an informal assessment, they need to establish specific goals for their own dialogue. These goals are typically derived directly from their observations of the inner circle. For example, if the first inner circle struggled to get balanced participation from all members, perhaps the outer circle will establish a goal that addresses that issue. These situations sometimes create opportunities for more Socratic questioning from the teacher, such as, How might we go about creating a more balanced level of participation? or What are some strategies we might use to accomplish this? Again, by using questioning and having students generate their own answers, they have an increased sense of ownership of the problem and of the solutions they choose to implement.

One of the problems that sometimes occurs with the goal-setting stage is that students may be tempted to create goals that are overly vague, such as, "We want to do a better job." The problem with generalized goals such as these is that it is difficult at the end of the process for students to know if they have been successful in meeting the goal. As a teacher, I might ask a follow-up question such as, How will we measure whether or not you have been successful with that goal? or How will we see your dialogue improve in this area? If students cannot produce answers to these questions, I ask them to go back and specify their goals, perhaps into "We want to do a better job by referencing the text more often." This has been very helpful in focusing student attention on clear and specific goals and has even led to some creative student problem solving. For example, many times a student will ask another student in the new outer circle to tally the number of references made to the text (or some similar behavior), and the inner circle will establish a target number to measure their accomplishment.

At the end of the class period, the goal-setting stage of the final outer circle takes on a new role. Since there will not be a new inner circle taking the place of the current one that day, the goals I ask the outer circle to establish are for the next Socratic circle and are more long range in nature. Oftentimes, students in the inner circle participate in this stage as well because our next groups will comprise different people. These long-term goals serve multiple purposes. First, they bring a sense of closure to the activity of the day. Some students are frustrated by the fact that their dialogue could seemingly continue on forever without reaching a conclusion or a sense of closure. The goals established in this final step (I sometimes refer to this as our debriefing session) help to bring that sense of closure and completion to the Socratic circle. Also, this debriefing session creates a link from one Socratic circle to another and reinforces the process of the activity and our striving for continuous improvement. Periodically, I ask one student to serve as our recorder and list these long-term goals on the chalkboard as a reminder during our next Socratic circle.

ENCOURAGING MORE MEANINGFUL FEEDBACK

Meaningful feedback from the outer circle is crucial to the success of not only an individual discussion but to the Socratic circle process as well. Without meaningful feedback the inner circle has a less clear idea of how well they did, and the class as a whole is not able to examine some of the behaviors and discussion skills that make Socratic circles successful. For students who struggle to offer meaningful feedback a teacher can do a number of things to encourage more thoughtful, constructive criticism.

One of the simplest ways to encourage more meaningful feedback is through praise. When a student makes a profound or insightful comment in the outer circle's discussion, the teacher should be sure to praise that student. The time is well spent and reinforces to all students the types of feedback the teacher is looking for. Although this may seem like an overly simple suggestion, the power of verbal praise within the outer circle's conversation is immense.

Another way to encourage more meaningful feedback from the outer circle is to place requirements on the comments. For example, I do not allow students to make broad generalities when we share our initial comments and observations. Students must be specific and detailed in explaining the strengths of the inner circle and some of the areas that could have been made better. I even encourage my students to comment on individual members of the inner circle by name. I also encourage students not to repeat the comments of another individual within the outer circle. However, I have noticed that it is important to vary the place in the circle where I start having students make their initial comments. Because I move student by student around the circle, students would be able to sit where they know they will be one of the first to share their ideas. But because I change the place within the circle where I start soliciting feedback, students are motivated to be as prepared as they can be.

I never shy away from asking students to expand upon their observations and feedback if I think they are being overly superficial in their critique of the inner circle's performance. Asking students to be more specific in their feedback and offer more constructive criticism helps to hold the students in the outer circle accountable, but also helps raise the quality of feedback to higher and higher levels. Also, when a student comments on one of the elements of the dialogue where I, too, want to focus attention, I may temporarily interrupt the flow of the outer circle and lead a side conversation about that particular element. These have been some of the most intense and beneficial moments of the outer circle. Students know that when I interrupt the flow of the initial observation and feedback circle, the point we are discussing is crucial. Students in both circles pay close attention, absorb the feedback, and make honest attempts at improvement.

What I have found particularly helpful in these short conversations when a particular element is identified is comparing the behavior we saw in that day's dialogue with similar behaviors we have seen in other dialogues. By establishing in student minds that a pattern of this behavior exists, they see more clearly the effects of this behavior over time. Likewise, I try to mention examples from previous dialogues in which this problem was avoided or controlled. Focusing student attention on this behavior over time provides them with multiple examples of its existence and helps them examine more closely the underlying reasons and causes of this behavior, so they can better understand the problem and brainstorm possible solutions.

By far the best strategy for helping the outer circle offer useful feedback and thereby helping the inner circle improve their dialogue is asking for specific suggestions and strategies for addressing identified weaknesses. For example, if students identify that a particular circle is having difficulty getting all of its members to participate and contribute to the dialogue, I will ask the outer circle to offer specific suggestions to correct the problem. In only a few seconds the entire class hears several possible strategies that can be used when this problem is encountered. Students are quick to implement these suggestions when needed, and because they come from peers, are more willing to try them. By offering strategies for improvement in addition to constructive criticism, students enhance the quality of their feedback and offer ideas that are more insightful and meaningful.

A final suggestion for improving the quality of feedback also serves as a follow-up activity. Occasionally after a Socratic circle, I have students in class write letters to the students in the other circle. I ask them to speak honestly and frankly about the feedback they were given and the degree to which it helped them better understand the quality of the conversation that took place. I also encourage students to mention specific comments made. Once students have turned these in and I have had a chance to look over them, I read selections from the letters aloud to the class and we discuss how the inner circle perceived and applied the feedback that was given. This strategy helps students see purpose and value in the work they do in the outside circle and reinforces the continuous process of improvement involved in Socratic circles.

MANAGING THE DYNAMICS OF THE OUTER CIRCLE

As with the inner-circle dialogue, once students learn the routine of the outer-circle feedback discussions, the strategy progresses smoothly with few problems. Students are aware of the task before them, are motivated to complete the task to the best of their ability, and are held accountable to their peers for their performance. Also like the inner circle, a few classroom management procedures can make the outer-circle discussion move successfully.

Keeping Students in the Outer Circle On-Task

Maintaining the interest and involvement of the outer circle is quite easy when the inner circle's dialogue is going well; however, when the conversation lags, keeping the outer circle on-task can be more difficult. Off-task behavior in the outer circle usually takes one of two forms: (1) students trying to whisper and hold their own conversations with one another (sometimes about the text itself), and (2) students engaged in some other activity (such as homework for another class, writing a note to a friend, or daydreaming).

One way to encourage students to take their role in the outer circle seriously is by requiring each one to make an initial comment or observation when the outer circle begins providing feedback. Because students know that they must speak intelligently about what has transpired before them, many are more motivated to pay closer and fuller attention to the dialogue. Being held accountable to one's peers is often reason enough for students to stay on-task.

Another method of keeping individual students in the outer circle on-task is to assign them a particular role within the group. This is primarily effective with students who have a chronic problem with attentiveness in the outer circle. Perhaps the student can be the recorder and take notes on the inner circle's discussion, or be the scorekeeper or mapmaker (see Chapter 8), or play any additional roles the teacher decides are productive for both the student and the class as a whole.

Students Who Over-Praise or Over-Criticize in the Outer Circle

Early in the Socratic circle process some students in the outer circle tend to praise the inner circle for what they do well but then trivialize or avoid discussing any of the areas the inner circle might improve upon to enhance their dialogue. Whether they are afraid of creating conflict with peers or are unaccustomed to and uncomfortable with commenting on group performance, helping students voice suggestions in a constructive manner—and be comfortable doing so—can greatly improve the overall quality of Socratic circles. Likewise, there occasionally are students who choose to criticize but never praise the inner circle for their dialogue. Although this happens far less frequently, these attitudes can cause great harm within a discussion. When students think they can't do anything to satisfy a specific person within the outer circle, that no amount of hard work or effort on their part will satisfy this person's concerns, they may think that abandoning Socratic circles altogether is a more viable option than continuing. There are, however, a number of effective ways to correct this.

One way to encourage students to offer constructive criticism is to model the idea for them on a consistent basis. By allowing students to see and hear examples of the teacher giving criticism of a constructive nature, students feel more comfortable expressing criticism of their own. Also, the teacher's phrasing and wording can provide examples of how students can be sensitive and considerate of their peers and their feelings. This strategy seems particularly effective early in the Socratic circle process, when students are still developing their comfort level with the activity. One danger in modeling criticism for students can be modeling too much; some students might think the teacher is being too obtrusive in the conversation and not allowing students in the outer circle to guide and direct the improvement of the inner circle themselves. Striking a fine balance between modeling and over-participation is important in stimulating students to examine the dialogue of the inner circle more critically.

A method of encouraging criticism on the part of the outer circle while leaving the conversation clearly grounded in student ideas is to have members of the outer circle write their suggestions anonymously on a piece of scratch paper. These written suggestions can then be collected by the teacher and read to the class without comments from the authors. The method is effective early in the process and can greatly help the members of each circle see examples of areas for improvement. I've noticed that students are not always as constructive with their comments when they are written anonymously as when they are spoken. At times when reading such anonymous comments, we pause and talk briefly as a class about how a specific criticism might be phrased in a more positive and constructive manner. This type of coaching on the outer circle's feedback can be very helpful and productive in improving Socratic circles but also is more time consuming than other methods. Like modeling, this strategy appears to work best in the first few Socratic circles as a way to teach the process and encourage and motivate students to reach their full potential.

Another strategy that avoids having the teacher be too vocal in the outer circle's conversation is to praise both students who praise and students who offer insightful comments of a more critical nature. Praising students both within the context of a Socratic circle and outside of the activity, whether after class or in the hallway, can be an excellent way to reinforce the class and individuals for their willingness to speak up and share an area for improvement with the inner circle. This appears to work best after the Socratic circle process has been established in the classroom and students are hitting an initial wall of resistance to moving the activity forward. Because the process can become repetitive for some students, finding ways to encourage and enhance the dialogue with more critical thinking as time progresses only helps to improve the Socratic circles themselves.

Also early in the Socratic circle process, when students are still new to the strategy, I occasionally ask those in the outer circle to name three strengths and one area for improvement as we travel around the outer circle soliciting feedback for the dialogue observed. This is effective in reinforcing the idea that there are always several things we do well in discussion and always a few areas in which we can improve. Although I am sometimes lenient with the level of specificity in the suggested area for improvement—for example, I might allow an overly general suggestion such as, "You need to talk more"—I require that students praise with as much specificity as they can muster, mentioning individual students and individual comments made within the dialogue. This reinforces for students the focus of the outer circle on helping the inner circle improve their dialogue and the idea that specific feedback is crucial. This strategy works best when I inform students in the outer circle ahead of time that they will need to offer three strengths and one area for improvement in their discussion. This helps them prepare more fully for the discussion and create better feedback for the inner circle.

Later in the Socratic circle process, I use the same strategy with the added stipulation that students in the outer circle cannot repeat any of the ideas offered by the students before them. This is more difficult and more time consuming but can be an excellent way of holding the students in the outer circle even more accountable for their careful observation and atten-tion to the dialogue of the inner circle. By holding students in the outer circle accountable for thinking of multiple students and examples of behavior that can be praised, the process of continuous growth is rein-forced and students learn that both praise and constructive criticism are necessary for it to occur.

A final way to enhance the quality of the outer circle's constructive feedback occurs during the final outer-circle discussion, or debriefing session. One of the topics I always try to guide the final conversation toward is whether or not the feedback of the outer circle has been helpful in improving the dialogue of the inner circle. By helping students see that the feedback being given, although perhaps difficult to offer and hear, is helping them to improve their discussion skills, they often embrace the debriefing sessions and the feedback itself. Often, individual students will praise one another for the suggestions they have made, either that day or in previous Socratic circles, and will explain how that suggestion has helped the group, usually offering specific classroom examples of which all students have knowledge. This type of praise from peers is very effective in increasing the frequency and quality of the outer circle's constructive criticism. When students know that their comments are valued by peers and useful in helping the class as a whole to improve, they grow more comfortable with the process and more willing to participate and contribute.

There are other ways of managing students who seem resolved to be overly critical or avoid criticism at all and who appear to find pleasure in disrupting the natural ebb and flow of the outer-circle discussion. Oftentimes, these students seem to enjoy having an audience. Disrupting the process of growth and the quest for improved dialogue is more interesting and challenging for them than participating in the activity at hand. Some students resist the collaborative and cooperative nature of Socratic circles, and seek to disrupt the activity as a means of exerting their individuality. After-class conferences can be successful in managing these types of problems. Removing the audience and discussing the student's performance one on one often can refocus the student and help him or her be more productive and participatory. During these conferences I sometimes offer the student options in how they participate.

At times, it is best to give these students a role in the outer circle that is different from his or her peers. Having that student take on the role of scorekeeper or mapmaker (see Chapter 8), or some similar role assigned by the inner circle, means the student can still be involved with the activity but at the same time be more individualistic. Although I would hesitate to have a student complete these tasks in dialogue after dialogue, I have noticed that occasional opportunities to assert his or her individuality offers the student a necessary outlet and allows him or her to be more productive and effective when in the more traditional outer-circle role.

Another strategy I have used is to remove the student from a particular Socratic circle and create an alternate assignment, usually focused on observing and commenting in writing on the dialogue of the inner circle. By having the student write an informal letter to me about his or her evaluation of the inner circle's dialogue, the student realizes just how many comments and suggestions he or she could make. But because the letter is written only for my eyes, the student also realizes that he or she has no opportunity to share those thoughts with the class. Oftentimes, a student given this task will ask me to read the letter to the class. I refuse. In a follow-up conference with the student, I explain that if the student wants an opportunity to share feedback with the class, he or she will have to follow the rules and procedures of the activity. This has been effective in motivating students to be productive members of the group and engage with the class in a more collaborative manner.

Managing the dynamics of the outer circle is an important role for the teacher in a Socratic circle. High-quality, constructive feedback helps the inner circle create better dialogue and helps students see a clearer purpose in the cooperative nature of both circles and the inherent continuous process of improvement. Although the outer circle's discussion is often quite basic in content, handling the personalities of the outer circle in a positive manner can produce more insightful and meaningful feedback and, ultimately, higher-quality dialogue.

CONCLUSION

The role of the outer circle is essential in supporting the idea of continuous growth through Socratic circles. Without the immediate feedback the outer circle provides to the inner circle, students would not have an opportunity to think reflectively, self-assess, and establish goals for future performance. As teachers, we can do a number of things in leading the discussion of the outer circle to make this process more effective and more fruitful for our students. Through our modeling, praise, Socratic questioning, and careful management of classroom behavior the outer circle can greatly assist the inner circle in improving the overall quality of dialogue and improve the thinking and discussion skills of all students.

Chapter 6

SOCRATIC CIRCLES IN ACTION

One of the best Socratic circles I have ever led—one that stimulated the greatest amount of student participation and the greatest variety of viewpoints—was on the opening two paragraphs of Zora Neale Hurston's *Their Eyes Were Watching God*, conducted with an American literature class of high school juniors. This dialogue was completed in March after students had been experiencing and learning from Socratic circles for the first three quarters of the school year. The twenty-five students in the class were all of average intelligence, represented a cross section of the student body, and would fit very well the description of a typical classroom full of sixteen- and seventeen-year-olds. However, one thing does separate this class—and this discussion—from others: these students demonstrate the very best of Socratic circles and the very best of the inquiry, exploration, and discovery that can take place when communities of learners (both the students and the teacher) allow these processes to take hold.

Below is the first half of this Socratic circle in its entirety. I have altered the language of the conversation slightly for the purposes of readability, but the ideas, thinking, and student questions are their own. Within the script of this conversation I have also included a few of my own reflections to highlight some of my thinking as the discussion leader and some of the lessons and skills I saw students developing and displaying over time.

> *Ships at a distance have every man's wish on board. For some they come in with the tide. For others they sail forever on the horizon, never out of sight, never landing until the Watcher turns his eyes away in resignation, his dreams mocked to death by Time. That is the life of men.*
>
> *Now, women forget all those things they don't want to remember, and remember everything they don't want to forget. The dream is the truth. Then they act and do things accordingly.*
> —Zora Neale Hurston, *Their Eyes Were Watching God*

COPELAND: As we get started with this circle, I'll offer you a starting point for your conversation. Obviously the message Hurston is conveying here is firmly grounded in metaphor. What do you see in your mind when you read these paragraphs? What images is Hurston painting for you? With that, inside circle, you have about ten minutes to discuss. Go.

[Each inner circle typically begins with a low-risk, open-ended question asked by the teacher or discussion leader. This type of question helps get the conversation moving and overcome the initial resistance to dialogue. It serves as a focal point until students identify their own topics and avenues of discussion they would like to explore.]

EMILY: Okay, well, when I read the first paragraph, I see a ship sitting in the ocean, not moving, not doing anything but sitting there. On board the ship is this guy who's dreaming of something, but he, too, is just sitting there doing nothing.

JOSH: Then what do you see in the second paragraph?

EMILY: That's just it. I don't see anything in my mind when I read the second paragraph. It's frustrating because I can see something so clearly at the beginning and then the whole thing just kind of disappears. Does anybody see anything in the second paragraph?

CAMIKA: I see a woman, but she's not doing anything, either, just like the guy. She's just sitting there watching the ship and the guy. I wonder if she is supposed to be the "Watcher" in the first paragraph.

TARYN: Yeah, I wrote down a question about that. Who is the Watcher? And why is the word capitalized?

CAMIKA: I wondered that, too.

EMILY: Anyone have any ideas?

[Already students have identified an area of interest and are beginning to explore that area using their own open-ended questions.]

TYLER: I was confused when I read it, but I thought the Watcher was the guy with the dream. You know, like he's "watching" for the dream to happen. But it didn't seem to make much sense to me.

DOMINIC: I thought the Watcher was God. [*momentary silence*]

DOMINIC: You know, because it's capitalized and all, just like God's name is capitalized. We even capitalize it when we refer to him as he.

TANISHA: I thought that, too, but I couldn't make any sense of it. "Time" is capitalized, too, and I was trying to figure out why. One of the things that I wrote down is that maybe there is a conflict going on here between God and Time. Like the man is in a race against time to ask God to make all of his dreams come true.

EMILY: That could be.

SCOTT: I agree with Tyler. I thought the Watcher was the guy with the dream.

TARYN: What made you think that?

SCOTT: Well, I disagree with Emily. When I picture this in my head, I don't see the man standing on the ship. I see him standing on the shoreline watching the ship. I think the ship itself is his dream but he feels helpless to go after it. All he can do is stand there and watch to see if his ship comes in or not.

EMILY: Isn't that a Billy Joel song?

TARYN: Who?

EMILY: Never mind, it's not important.

[Students often make personal connections to the text based on experiences from their own lives. Here, Emily connects the discussion to "Uptown Girl," a song by Billy Joel. After this dialogue when I asked Emily about this reference, she mentioned that her mother often listens to his music. I asked Emily if she could connect the content of this song to our discussion in any way; at that moment she could not. The next day in class, however, she brought in the lyrics and spent several minutes explaining how the song was "just like what Hurston wrote." Teachers can encourage students to make personal connections to the text and such comparisons as a way of analyzing and exploring meaning.]

TARYN: Okay. [*to Scott*] So what made you think the man was standing on the beach?

SCOTT: The line "For some, they come in with the tide." If the ship is just out there floating, the tide might carry it in to shore and it might not. All the guy can do is wait and see. The only question is whether he is patient enough to wait for it or not.

TARYN: That makes sense, I guess.

CAMIKA: It makes sense with the next line, too. "For others they sail forever on the horizon, never out of sight, never landing until the Watcher turns his eyes away in resignation, his dreams mocked to death by Time."

TYLER: Well, duh, that's why the second sentence starts "For some" and the third sentence starts "For others." It's like two halves of the same whole there.

CAMIKA: Fine, sorry.

COPELAND: Good, Tyler, I'm glad you pointed that out—although I think you could have found a more polite way to express it without crushing Camika's feelings. What are these two halves Tyler is talking about?

[Here I interrupt the conversation to offer constructive criticism on the civility of the dialogue. This serves three purposes: (1) to intervene in a positive manner before the disrespectful attitude gets out of hand and affects the quality of the conversation, (2) to reinforce to all students that Camika did nothing wrong, and (3) to identify a behavior upon which the students in the outer circle might focus their attention. Redirecting the offending comment in the form of a question then revives the conversation.]

EMILY: It's what happens to men's dreams. Some of them come true and some of them don't.

COPELAND: Good. And what is it that makes some of them come true and some of them not come true?

EMILY: [to Copeland] The tide.

COPELAND: Remember, talk to each other, not to me.

[Students often have a difficult time breaking the habits of more traditional classroom discussion, where all comments are directed toward the teacher. I find this especially common after I have interrupted their dialogue. Simply reminding the students of the purpose here is often enough to correct the problem.]

EMILY: The tide. [class laughs] It's like fate. Some dreams come true, some don't.

TANISHA: I don't know. I don't think so. It says, "never landing until the Watcher turns his eyes away in resignation, his dreams mocked to death by Time." All the ships come to land, all the dreams come true; it's just a question of whether or not the man has given up on his dream.

TYLER: I don't get what you mean.

TANISHA: It's like the moment a guy gives up on his dream, the moment he "turns his eyes away in resignation," that's the moment the dream finally comes true, but the guy has left and isn't looking for it anymore and totally misses it.

TYLER: That's a little depressing, don't you think?

TANISHA: That's what it says.

SCOTT: What does "resignation" mean? Did anyone look it up?

EMILY: I did. It means, "the act or an instance of resigning." And when I looked up "resign," it said, "to submit oneself passively or to accept as inevitable."

SCOTT: So, basically, it is fate. The guy gives up because it is never meant to be. He turns away from his dream because he knows it is never going to happen.

TANISHA: I still don't think so. He still gives up on his dream, and if he would have waited just a little bit longer he would have gotten it. It's more like luck. If the guy would have waited longer, his luck would have changed and he would have found his dream.

SCOTT: So what's the difference between luck and fate?

TANISHA: Fate will happen; it's only a matter of time and there's nothing anyone can do to change what's going to happen. With luck there is more of a question of what is going to happen, like not everything is so decided. Some things happen and some things don't, depending on the circumstances. With fate, it either happens for sure or it doesn't happen for sure.

EMILY: So what is it about this situation that makes you think it's luck and not fate?

TANISHA: I don't know. I guess it's just that the guy should have waited a bit longer and not turned around so soon. If he would have, maybe that ship would have come to shore and he could have gotten his dream.

TYLER: There you go again, bashing on the guys.

TANISHA: How am I bashing on the guys?

TYLER: You keep saying that we don't wait for dreams, that we stand around and just count on our luck to make things happen. It's like you think we're stupid or something.

TANISHA: I'm just explaining what I see in the text. I'm not bashing anyone.

[Teaching students to use the text as evidence and support for their arguments is critically important. Many students find the text itself to be a form of safety net during their dialogue. Because the text is in front of them, it serves as a tangible reminder of what is truly known and undeniable.]

EMILY: But maybe the author is.

TYLER: What?

EMILY: Maybe that's what the author is trying to say. Maybe she's saying that that's what guys are like. They give up too easily on their dreams.

TYLER: You really believe that?

EMILY: It's a possibility. I can see what Tanisha means about the luck thing, though. I think she's right—there does seem to be some blaming of guys going on here for not going after their dreams.

TYLER: I don't agree with that.

TANISHA: Why not?

TYLER: I just think that if there's any blaming going on here, it's blaming the women.

EMILY: Okay, but why don't you see any possibility of blame on the men?

TYLER: I just don't.

[Although the point of a Socratic circle is to work collaboratively in search of the truth, differences in opinion and disagreement can be a positive element in any conversation.]

SCOTT: I see what you guys are saying. Guys would be better off if they would be more patient and maybe their dreams would come true. I can agree with that. I don't think anyone's dreams are handed to them. I'm not sure it's luck involved so much as work, but I think that giving up on your dreams definitely kills them.

DOMINIC: Yeah, that's true. It's still true today. Some people are willing to work for their dreams and some aren't. Those that aren't willing to work for them just sit around expecting someone to hand them to them. Most of the time they just give up on the dream and get bitter about the whole situation.

JOSH: I like that idea. That sounds pretty good to me. I think we've figured it out.

[Josh, like many students, appears content to take the first real insight of the dialogue as the one and only "correct answer." Over time students learn through Socratic circles not to be satisfied with insights that arise first. Often, deeper, more meaningful insight will reveal itself as the dialogue continues and intensifies.]

TARYN: Okay, well, we've talked a lot about the first paragraph—what about the second? What is she [Hurston] saying there?

EMILY: Camika, earlier you said that you see a woman when you read the second paragraph. What do you think she [Hurston] is talking about?

CAMIKA: I think the second paragraph is weird. I still kind of think that the woman is the Watcher, but I'm not exactly sure why. It's almost like the woman is laughing at the man.

TANISHA: What do you mean?

[One of the early lessons for students in Socratic circles is that they must listen to and thoroughly comprehend the comments made by their peers. Because this strategy involves the collaborative construction of understanding, students who are not following along mentally with the ideas of their partners will be of no benefit to the group while their peers in the outer circle watch. Students learn quickly to ask questions of each other and clarify when they are unsure of what was meant.]

CAMIKA: Well, let's face it, guys dream some pretty silly dreams sometimes. They all think they're going to play in the NBA or be a rock star or a millionaire. They always dream great big things that are never going to happen.

TYLER: Oh, and girls never dream ridiculous dreams, is that what you're saying?

CAMIKA: No, but I do think there is a difference in the kinds of dreams that men dream and the kinds of dreams women dream about.

TARYN: Men do have a tendency to dream about great big things, while most girls dream about smaller things.

JOSH: I don't know that I agree with that. But I think girls dream just as many wild dreams as guys do. I mean, come on, aren't women supposed to be just as good as men these days in everything they do? Why should dreams be any different?

CAMIKA: That's true, but I think you have to keep in mind when this was written. I mean, the lives of women have changed quite a bit since then.

COPELAND: You bring up a great point, Camika. Obviously Hurston is writing from a perspective in her own time period, the 1930s. Life has changed quite a bit since then for both men and women. And the experiences of an African American woman in the 1930s would be even more different than the experiences of an African American woman today. But even though this writing is more than sixty years old, is there still some truth to this idea?

[Here I interrupt the conversation again because I think students are developing too many different avenues of conversation and to praise Camika for reflecting on the writing's time period and the reference to the importance of change over time. As teachers and discussion leaders monitor the dialogue, it is important to help students keep their conversation moving forward and explore the ideas behind the text and not to reduce the dialogue to mere directionless debate. Again, I do this here by posing another open-ended question to refocus the circle on the task at hand.]

TARYN: I think there is. In some ways, guys and girls are just different. One way isn't necessarily better than the other; they're just different. It's like what it says here, "women forget all those things they don't want to remember, and remember everything they don't want to forget." Guys hang on to their dreams and try to wait patiently for those dreams to come true. If a girl's dream doesn't come true, she just moves on to another dream that she thinks will.

EMILY: I can see that. Like it says, "The dream is the truth."

TYLER: So, girls just dream about the things they can already have? Is that what you're saying? [pause]

EMILY: I don't understand what you're asking.

TYLER: It says, "The dream is the truth." If it's already the truth, why do you need to dream about it? You've already got it.

TARYN: Maybe they don't realize they've already got it. Maybe one of the things that makes guys and girls different is that girls actually take the time to understand and appreciate the dreams that they do have, whereas guys just waste their time and keep on dreaming about the things they don't.

CAMIKA: That would make sense. It does say, "Then they act and do things accordingly." Girls work for their dreams. Guys don't.

DOMINIC: That does fit in with what we talked about earlier, with some people being willing to work for their dreams and some people being willing to sit around and wait for someone to hand it to them.

TYLER: So what this is saying is that men just sit around and do nothing while women do all of the work!

TARYN: Not really. It's deeper than that. Men are so busy doing the actual dreaming that they never take any action to make the dream happen. While women actually try to make their dreams come true.

JOSH: But men dream bigger dreams. They can't take any action to move something as big as a ship! Women can work to make their dreams happen because they dream so much smaller dreams.

CAMIKA: Whoa! I don't dream small dreams; I dream as big dreams as anyone. Don't even try to suggest that women can't dream as big as men.

JOSH: I'm not saying that; it's what is written here.

CAMIKA: Where? Show me. Where does it say that women can't dream as big as men.

JOSH: It's not that they *can't*. It's that they *don't*.

CAMIKA: Fine. Where does it say they *don't* dream as big as men?

[Here again the text itself serves as a resource for students to pull evidence and support for their ideas and also grounds the dialogue taking place.]

JOSH: [*referring to the text*] Well, okay, maybe it doesn't. It just says that "the dream is the truth," like saying that women only dream of things they believe they can make happen. What do you think, Taryn?

TARYN: I'm not so sure about that. All that's really saying is that women are more realistic in their dreams than men.

DOMINIC: You know, that's kind of right. That's the way it was in *The Great Gatsby*, too. Gatsby wanted to turn back the clock and make everything perfect. Daisy just wanted happiness like right here, right now. Her dream was much more realistic. And Gatsby never really did much to make his dream happen. He just stood there staring at that dumb green light.

[Like personal connections, intertextual connections provide students an opportunity to make comparisons between prior knowledge and new learning. Here, Dominic connects the message of the opening paragraphs of *Their Eyes Were Watching God* to *The Great Gatsby* and comments on their similarity. These connections not only expand the scope of the learning that is currently taking place, but also help reinforce the learning that has already occurred.]

COPELAND: I hate to cut you off when you're in the middle of some awfully good stuff, but your time is up. Can someone in the inner circle quickly summarize the conversation that just took place?

[Asking for a brief summary of the conversation is often an effective method for accomplishing two goals: (1) it helps to reinforce in the minds of the students in the inner circle what was accomplished in their dialogue, and (2) it signals to the members of the outer circle that the time for their feedback is approaching and gives them a moment to collect their thoughts.]

EMILY: Basically we talked about how men and women differ in the way they approach chasing their dreams.

COPELAND: Good. Can anyone add to this summary?

TARYN: We talked about who works harder for their dreams and who dreams the bigger dreams. And also who has the dreams that are more realistic.

JOSH: And Dominic helped us to connect it to *Gatsby*.

COPELAND: Excellent. Now let's go once around the outside and hear some of the initial feedback and observations from the outer circle. Austin, you're first.

[Initially I begin the conversation of the outer circle with a quick trip "around the world" to hear from each student in sequential order. Every student is required to make a few comments about the behavior they observed in the inner circle. Because students in the inner circle know this feedback is coming, they are held accountable while they are discussing the text. I have also found that requiring reluctant students to speak in the outer circle increases their comfort level and makes them more likely to contribute when they are in the inner circle.]

AUSTIN: Overall I was really impressed by the conversation of the inner circle. They asked good questions and did a great job of using the text to support their answers. There was some healthy disagreement, but they focused on the text and used that disagreement to better understand what was going on. There were a few people who didn't say anything and I would have liked to have seen the group try to include those people more.

JALEN: I thought they did a great job, too. They really stayed focused on the text and the topic and brought up ideas that I had never even thought about. I was impressed.

WILL: I agree with Jalen. They did a good job. This was probably one of the best Socratic circles we've done all semester long. It seems like they discovered everything there is to discover here. I'm not sure there's anything left for us to discuss.

COPELAND: That's an interesting thought, Will. But we've said that before and always been shocked at what the second group has come up with. I'm willing to bet today will be no different. How about you, Megan, what did you observe?

MEGAN: It was definitely a good conversation, but I was bothered by a couple of things. One, the disagreement and arguing was a little rude and I think what Tyler said to Camika probably affected her willingness to contribute to the group. After he said that, she didn't say another thing until Emily pulled her back into the conversation toward the end. The other thing that bothered me was that Sarah, Michael, Kathy, and Christina didn't say anything and the group didn't even seem to notice or care.

COPELAND: Outstanding point, Megan—we'll come back to that in a minute. Tara, how about you? What did you see and observe?

TARA: Yeah, obviously they did a good job, just like everyone has said already. But I was kind of bored with the conversation. It just didn't seem that interesting to me.

COPELAND: Well, Tara, their goal and purpose in this conversation wasn't to keep you entertained, but to explore the text and the ideas behind it. Did you notice anything specific about how this group performed?

[Here I interrupt the flow of the feedback session to correct a misperception of the reasons for having a Socratic circle and refocus the outer circle on their role. This type of coaching is continually necessary, regardless of how experienced students are with the process.]

TARA: [*after a short pause while thinking*] I thought Emily did a good job of leading the discussion. She kept the conversation moving forward and did a good job of keeping everybody focused on the text.

COPELAND: Good, much better job of providing feedback. What about you, Serina?

SERINA: I thought they did an awesome job—by far the best Socratic circle we've done all year. They really dug deep and pulled out some pretty cool stuff. I thought Emily and Taryn were good leaders for the group and helped move the conversation along.

AMAYA: Me, too. They did a good job, but it seemed like the conversation was basically between about four people and then a few others made a couple of comments and the rest just sat there. There wasn't much balance to the conversation. Caroline looked totally lost, like she wasn't even paying attention. She just sat there poking holes in her paper.

TYRONE: I agree with pretty much everything that has been said. Everyone did good. I liked how the conversation stayed on-topic and didn't get sidetracked. I liked how they talked about the first paragraph thoroughly and then moved on to the second paragraph.

CHRIS: Yeah, they did good. They focused an awful lot on the guy, but they didn't talk about the girls hardly at all. But other than that they did real good.

COPELAND: Chris, can you come up with any ways or any strategies that the inner circle might have used so that they spent equal time talking about men's dreams and women's dreams?

CHRIS: I don't know. Maybe . . . [*thinking*] I don't know, I can't come up with anything.

COPELAND: That's okay. Maybe this is an area your group can work on here in a minute when we switch circles. You did a good job of identifying a potential weakness. Now that we've acknowledged it, maybe we can find a way to improve it.

[Here I focus on helping Chris, a student who struggles with Socratic circles and class in general, find success within the context of what we've done. Some students are naturally better in this setting than others. The feedback session of the outer circle provides a good opportunity to coach struggling students while at the same time identifying and modeling for the other students the process of dialogue improvement.]

COPELAND: What feedback can you offer, Stephanie?

STEPHANIE: I thought it was really interesting to watch how the guys and girls within the group behaved. When the girls talked about the dreams of guys, the guys in the group got all defensive and accused Tanisha of bashing on them. Then at the end when the group was talking about the dreams of women, the guys were the ones that were bashing on the girls for having small dreams.

JESSICA: I agree with Stephanie, but what was real interesting to me is that when the guys accused the girls of bashing on the guys, the girls could point to the place in the text where their ideas were coming from. But when Camika challenged the guys to use the text to defend their ideas, they couldn't do it.

COPELAND: That's an excellent point. And again we see that using the text to support your argument is critical to having the group find validity in your ideas. I'm glad to see you paid attention to that, Jessica. How about you, Aeisha, what did you notice about their conversation?

AEISHA: I don't know. I think everyone has already said everything there is to say. There's no more to add.

COPELAND: Can you think of at least one specific strength or area for improvement that hasn't been mentioned yet?

AEISHA: Well, they should've done a better job of trying to get the quiet people to talk. They didn't really do anything to make them want to talk or even give them a chance to say anything even if they wanted to.

[Once the initial feedback stage of the outer circle's conversation has finished, we begin to examine some of the ideas mentioned more closely. This portion of the feedback session is much more teacher directed and more similar to traditional forms of classroom discussion. It is at this stage that most discussion skills coaching occurs.]

COPELAND: Great. Now let's go back through some of these ideas and talk about a couple of them in a little more detail. What were the obvious strengths of this group?

JALEN: They did a good job of focusing on the text and using it within their conversation. They kept the conversation organized and on-topic. And they got deep into the meaning of what the author was tying to say.

COPELAND: Yes, I would agree. The group did a superb job with all three of those things. Were there specific strategies the group used that allowed those things to occur or did they just happen at random? Tara, what do you think?

TARA: Well, obviously the group was well prepared and that makes a huge difference in the quality of the conversation that is taking place. I mean, if you look over people's shoulders, you can see how much they have written down on their papers. I think that makes a huge difference.

COPELAND: Well said. And let's keep in mind, is it important exactly what they write down?

SERINA: No, like we've talked about before, what you write down is merely a sign of how much thought you've put into the text and how well you've prepared for the discussion.

COPELAND: Excellent. What did this group do that helped to keep their conversation so organized and on-topic?

AMAYA: Like Tyrone said, taking the text one paragraph at a time and discussing the dreams of men before moving on to women's dreams was a good way to stay on-task. I think that probably helped them dig deeper into the text as well.

COPELAND: What makes you say that, Amaya?

AMAYA: It just makes sense. If the group is more organized and on-task, then more people are probably following along and are paying attention to the conversation. When that happens, more people are likely to participate and the conversation is more likely to go farther.

COPELAND: You bet. Are there other reasons this conversation seemed to progress farther than some of our others?

MEGAN: Well, this was definitely a piece of text that everybody could get into. I mean, everybody has dreams and I think we're all interested in making our dreams come true. If this lady has some secret on how to make our dreams happen, I think we'd all listen.

COPELAND: Well said.

JESSICA: I think the arguing helped, too.

COPELAND: Explain what you mean, Jessica.

JESSICA: Well, I mean, I was sitting here in the outside circle and I felt the adrenaline rush when the guys started saying that women don't dream as big as men. I'm sure the girls on the inside circle felt it, too. It made me want to jump in there and throw in my two cents. And I'm pretty sure the guys felt the same way when us girls were saying they were stupid for always sitting around and waiting for their dreams to come true.

COPELAND: Another excellent point. Good. Now let's focus on some of the areas of this conversation that could have been improved. What did you see that could have been made better?

[In addition to focusing on the strengths of the inner circle's discussion behavior, we always spend a few moments focusing on areas for improvement. Although sometimes difficult for the inner circle to quietly endure, this reflection provides instant feedback on the inner circle's performance and allows both groups to better understand what has transpired.]

STEPHANIE: Four of their twelve members never said a word.

COPELAND: Yes, this is an obvious area of concern. Like we've talked about all year long, every person and every idea matters. Even if you are throwing out what you consider to be a dumb idea, it may spark an idea in the mind of someone else that leads the group to an epiphany. What could this group have done to include a greater number of voices?

CHRIS: Go after people more.

COPELAND: Explain what you mean, Chris.

CHRIS: Ask more questions. Don't let them off the hook so easy. Don't let them just sit there like a bump on a log.

COPELAND: That's certainly one way to handle it. Are there other strategies that might work as well, perhaps ways to encourage people to participate rather than forcing them to participate?

TYRONE: We've talked about asking the person, What do you think? Maybe even better than that would be to ask them something specific. Something like, Do you agree with what is said in this line? That way they can't come back with something like, "I don't know."

COPELAND: That's a great idea. Starting off with a simple, low-risk question so that the person speaking can build a little confidence. Maybe it is even a close-ended, yes/no question. Once the person has answered, you could always follow up with another question to have them explain why. I think that is a great idea. Other areas for improvement that we can identify?

MEGAN: The arguing that took place could have been better. It seemed like a number of people in the circle got defensive when their ideas were challenged. I'm not really sure if there is a way to fix it, but it did seem to affect the conversation.

COPELAND: Sometimes dialogue does move us out of our comfort zones. Can anyone think of a way that we could exchange and challenge each other's ideas without feeling as though we are being challenged as people?

AUSTIN: I think that's almost impossible to do. At some point every person will feel challenged. But what we have to keep in mind is those challenges are to help the group discover the truth.

STEPHANIE: I think just keeping the golden rule in mind is a good idea, too. If we all just try to imagine being on the receiving end of the challenge we are making before we speak, I think we're more likely to be more polite in how we do it.

COPELAND: Good. That's a strong point and something we all should try to keep in mind. Okay, outside circle, on that scale of one to ten, how did this group do? [*A chorus of voices offers numbers from six to nine.*] It sounds as though I'm hearing an average of about an eight. Will, can you justify that rating for the inside circle?

[Asking for a numeric rating on a scale of one to ten allows both groups to compare this performance to previous experiences and gives the inner circle an additional type of instant feedback about the quality of their performance. The justification of the rating again allows the outer circle to summarize their findings and reinforces in the minds of the inner circle the validity of the rating.]

WILL: Basically, they had a good conversation that focused on the text and pulled out a lot of meaning, but they could have gotten more people involved and been more polite within the conversation.

COPELAND: Outstanding. Okay, outside circle, what goals do you want to establish for your conversation?

SERINA: Encourage more people to be involved and get them to talk.

COPELAND: Good. Any others?

WILL: Continue digging deeper into the text and discovering more meaning.

COPELAND: Great, let's go with those. Okay, switch circles and let's get the conversation going again.

[The conversation of the outer circle ends with establishing goals for their turn in the inner circle. This helps to establish in the minds of students specific areas to work on improving and increases discussion skills. This goal setting allows the new outer circle to have specific areas upon which to focus their attention as well.]

With preparation and practice student dialogue such as this can become a classroom reality. Our democratic society strives to include the voices and opinions of all stakeholders, to build consensus and purpose through open minds and conversation. Socratic circles offer students real-world practice in this very process and enable the discovery of voice and ownership of ideas. When students can be empowered to be responsible for their own growth and learning, great things can occur. Not only are curricular skills such as reading, writing, speaking, listening, critical thinking, and creativity expanded and enhanced, but social skills such as conflict resolution, team building, and collaboration are also improved.

Many of my students have come back to me years after leaving my classroom and thanked me for the opportunities of learning Socratic circles provide. They report overwhelmingly that the skills of critical reading that they developed through Socratic circles have directly affected their success in both their postsecondary education and their chosen careers. Because the process of critical reading and critical thinking was modeled for them, because they were provided with an opportunity to develop their own thinking and reasoning, because a philosophy was encouraged where questions themselves have as much relevance as the answers they produce, my students thought they had a firmer grasp on the higher-order thinking that colleges and employers were asking them to use. With the positive, supportive climate that Socratic circles create, students are able to develop their skills at their own pace with a sense of confidence and support from others.

Chapter 7

ALIGNING SOCRATIC CIRCLES WITH THE CURRICULUM

DIALOGUE INSPIRED BY JULIA CAMERON'S *The Right to Write.*

ASHLEY: *In the second paragraph, she writes, "In our current culture, writing is not forbidden; it is discouraged. Hallmark does it for us. We shop for the card that is 'closest' to what we wish to say." Do you guys agree with her or not?*

CHRIS: *I do. That's one of the reasons I hate buying cards for people. They never say exactly what you want them to and you're stuck with whatever is inside. Half the time it's something stupid.*

ERIC: *So why don't you just make your own?*

CHRIS: *Usually I do. That way it means what I want it to. I hate getting a card from someone when it's obvious what's written inside isn't something that person would ever say or think.*

AMBER: *Don't you think that's her main point? We're all human and we have all these thoughts and feelings, but we're horrible at expressing them. In school we get so bogged down in rules and grammar and proving our ideas that we forget how to express ourselves. I can't remember the last time that I wrote something in school that actually meant something to me and came from my heart. Sorry, Mr. Copeland.*

COPELAND: *I see your point. Is there anyplace in the text where you see Cameron making the same argument?*

AMBER: *I think in that same paragraph where she says, "Writing, as we are taught to do it, becomes an antihuman activity. We are forever editing, leaving out the details that might not be pertinent. We are trained to self-doubt, to self-scrutiny in the place of self-expression." It's like teachers have to make everything about right answers and wrong answers, instead of just letting us think and feel sometimes.*

NICK: *I'm not sure I agree with that. I think schools should be teaching us about punctuation and topic sentences and transitions and stuff. That's what is going to help me be successful when I get a job. I don't care as much about expressing my feelings.*

ASHLEY: *But what about those of us who do care about expressing our feelings? Don't we deserve an opportunity to do so? I agree with Amber. Schools try to kill our creativity.*

NICK: *You can be creative at home. Besides, we get a lot more freedom to write about what we want to in this class than we did in most of my other English classes. Even with the formal essay we just finished, we still could choose which topic to write about, and the argument we wanted to make, and which quotations we used to make our point.*

ASHLEY: *But what would have happened if one of us decided that we didn't want to use quotations to prove our point? What if we wanted to share something personal from our own life that helped prove a point about a character? We wouldn't pass, and we'd have to rewrite it anyway.*

AMBER: *See, that proves my point. Schools just want all to do things the same way. They want us all to be the same. There's no room for personality or freedom or anything else.*

Now that the *what* and *how* have been explained, teachers must consider the *why* and *when* of Socratic circles. Within the curriculum of any given school or any given class, there is ample room to incorporate this strategy. Despite the fact that this text focuses primarily on the use of Socratic circles within English language arts at the middle school and high school level, the pedagogy here can be applied to almost any content area and can be adapted to any age group. At the heart of the curriculum of any class in any content area is the goal of instilling in students the knowledge and skills necessary to grow personally and develop into productive and responsible citizens. In the modern classroom, with our focus on outcomes, objectives, and assessment, we sometimes lose track of our purpose in education—to create productive citizens capable of leading meaningful and successful lives in a rapidly changing world. Socratic circles help students see value and purpose in classroom learning and help them make connections between learning that occurs in the classroom and plans for their own futures.

Great debate has taken place recently about the value and importance of two distinct types of curriculum: content-based curriculum and skills-based curriculum. Programs such as the E. D. Hirsch–inspired Cultural Literacy movement seek to reinforce the idea that there is a body of common knowledge all students should recognize and be able to recall to understand the many avenues of written and oral communication in our society. As Hirsch (1993) suggests, reading is a far more complex task than simply knowing the denotative meanings of words and phrases. There is a great deal of background knowledge that writers assume readers know. Understanding this content-based knowledge is crucial to higher levels of learning and therefore to life success.

Others suggest that students' learning time is not best spent in memorizing facts and data but in practicing the skills necessary for acquiring that content knowledge on their own, that teaching the skills and processes of reading are far more important than teaching the content within a selection of text. The old adage "Give a man a fish and you feed him for a day; teach a man to fish and you feed him for a lifetime" mirrors this thinking.

Although great time and effort can be spent showing examples that suggest one side of this debate carries more weight and importance than the other, most would agree that high-quality teaching provides students opportunities to engage in both of these styles of learning. To be best prepared for the future, students need thorough understanding of the common knowledge members of western culture draw upon, and practice in developing strong skills in learning and communication processes. Socratic circles provide just such an opportunity. We see expression of this very idea in the work of Mortimer Adler.

ADLER'S THREE COLUMNS OF LEARNING

Writing on behalf of the members of the Paideia Group, a group of educational thinkers and policy makers concerned about the future of public education in America, Mortimer Adler described The Three Columns of Learning in *The Paideia Proposal: An Educational Manifesto* (1982). Adler's proposed interconnected columns are essential to student learning and represent both different styles of teaching and different styles of learning. Adler titles Column One "Acquisition of Knowledge," which includes all of the content and factual information a teacher conveys to students, much like the E. D. Hirsch–inspired Cultural Literacy movement. Column Two, "Development of Skill," provides opportunities to demonstrate the intellectual skills of learning that students are expected to be successful in, much like our use of behavioral outcomes and performance indicators. The learning that occurs in Column Two is *know-how*, the ability to *do* and *perform*, whereas learning in Column One is *knowledge about*, knowing the *facts* of a given topic or subject.

Columns One and Two are quite similar to the division of content-based and skills-based curriculum. However, Adler extended his vision of learning with a third column, "Enlargement of the Understanding," that goes well beyond the current debate about a content-based versus a skills-based curriculum. Adler proposed that students be given an opportunity to synthesize information and skills from Columns One and Two and to practice the real-world skills of group inquiry, critical thinking, and problem solving. Instruction in Column Three advances with maieutic teaching—Socratic questioning and students' active participation in discussion of artistic works, whether written, created, or performed. The Socratic method of learning embodied by Column Three allows students to use the skills they have developed in Column Two—reading, thinking, speaking, listening—while applying the facts and content learned in Column One to new learning. By drawing on prior knowledge and classroom experience, students can discuss their ideas and values and enhance their learning. In this way, students can "raise their minds up from a state of understanding or appreciating less to a state of understanding or appreciating more" (p. 29).

Adler's Three Columns of Learning suggest a manner and method in which Socratic circles can be added to the curriculum of any class. Socratic circles are one of a multitude of strategies that teachers have at their fingertips; certainly, no one should embrace this strategy so wholeheartedly as to engage in it daily and abandon the other worthwhile activities that transpire in a classroom. Our classrooms should continue to be centers of diverse learning activities all suited to best prepare students for the future. Without the content and skills instruction described by Adler in Columns One and Two, the value, worth, and importance of Socratic circles will never come to life in the minds of our students. However, by weaving Socratic circles into our classrooms throughout our other units, objectives, and activities, we can enhance and expand student learning.

PLACING SOCRATIC CIRCLES WITHIN THE CURRICULUM

Understanding that Socratic circles have a viable role in the general school curriculum is an important first step, but understanding where teachers can implement dialogue in a particular class or with a particular group of students is equally important. Teachers often struggle to find the time and the place to squeeze new activities into their pedagogy, asking important questions such as, With which classes and students do I use this idea? How often do I use this strategy? and How do I connect a specific Socratic circle to what my class is already learning? These are important questions for teachers and can be answered only when considering the specifics of each teacher, class, and classroom; however, there are several general principles that can make this process far easier.

Despite common misperceptions, Socratic teaching and learning is not a process that should be reserved for honors students or students bound for postsecondary study. In fact, some of the most insightful dialogue that has blossomed in my classroom has come from students with the least amount of academic interest. Because student-centered dialogue is generated from the prior knowledge and experience of the participants, and because it is a collaborative activity that requires students to work together to construct group understanding and meaning, the strategy can be applied to the broadest range of classes.

Some teachers believe that students who are not labeled as gifted or are not bound for college are simply not capable of discussing ideas of a philosophical nature. All students are capable of sharing ideas with their peers and of generating new ideas based on those shared by others. And for this reason alone, any group of students could benefit from the dialogue opened through this strategy. All students deserve the opportunity to find their voices and consider the ideas and values that shape our lives and our futures. In fact, lower-achieving students seem to benefit the most from this approach to learning. The voice and ownership created through the application of Socratic circles establishes a stronger sense of purpose and relevance for the learning that occurs.

As bridging the achievement gap between higher-performing and lower-performing students becomes more of a priority in schools, finding methods and strategies that motivate and inspire students will continue to grow in importance. In my experience and in the experience of other teachers I work with who use this type of student dialogue, the most growth has occurred in our academically challenged classes. The sense of curiosity and habits of critical thought instilled through Socratic circles can help make learning more personal and relevant to the lives of students for whom education and learning are more of a struggle.

Frequency of Scheduling

It has been my experience that Socratic circles progress more smoothly and produce greater results when they are scheduled on a consistent and predictable basis. When students know about and can prepare for dialogue, they enter the classroom with a different attitude and purpose. Scheduling Socratic circles in advance, with text students can relate to their own lives, and that mirrors or expands upon what the class is currently learning are all critical to their success. Socratic circles should never be scheduled and text should never be chosen without a great deal of forethought and planning.

Obviously, Socratic circles should not take place in the classroom 100 percent of the time or even on a daily basis; they are not suitable for teaching content knowledge. However, the level of skills development and critical thinking that Socratic circles can facilitate with information previously taught is amazing. They allow students to use higher-order thinking skills, creativity, and problem-solving strategies that lead groups to a higher understanding of ultimate truth through making connections and drawing comparisons to learning already assimilated. These connections and comparisons open many doors to cross-curricular learning as well.

Adler proposes that all students within a given school have the opportunity to participate in a Socratic circle at least once a week. Adler also suggests that this strategy works best if all students within that school are engaging in dialogue about the same piece of text on the same day at the same time—an idea he refers to as the Wednesday Revolution. In that way, students can compare and contrast the dialogue held in one classroom with the dialogue held in another classroom and ultimately gain exposure to a broader range of ideas shared by a wide variety of people.

Based on my own experience, I would agree with Adler that Socratic circles are most effective when held on a regular basis. Continual application of the strategy on a predictable schedule helps students feel more comfortable with the process and allows them to make honest and forthright attempts at growth and improvement over time, especially when Socratic circles are first introduced.

For students new to Socratic circles it can be helpful to schedule the activity more often than once a week, although I never schedule Socratic circles on back-to-back days. Students need time to process the dialogue they have experienced and to take to heart the feedback and goals they have received and established for themselves. Scheduling dialogue for consecutive class periods only frustrates students, and they can begin to believe that dialogue is something being *done to* them, rather than *done through* them. Too-frequent Socratic circles can undermine the very sense of ownership and voice that student-centered dialogue seeks to create. Likewise, waiting too long between Socratic circles can lead to problems in overcoming that initial awkward or uncomfortable feeling with the strategy itself. The vast majority of my classes take three to four Socratic circles to fully explore the possibilities of the strategy and work through the initial obstacles of productive classroom dialogue. I typically schedule these first Socratic circles within a two-week period, usually on Tuesdays and Thursdays. This permits time between each activity for students to reflect and consider alternatives but does not allow so much that students forget the learning that took place within the previous dialogue.

Once those initial Socratic circles have been completed and students are familiar and comfortable with the process, I rarely schedule more than one per week, especially if multiple teachers within the school are using the activity with their classes. Some students grow tired with and feel burdened by over-exposure to Socratic circles. They require a good deal of effort and mental work, and some students are unaccustomed to being asked to actively participate in class on a consistent basis. Scheduling Socratic circles too frequently can actually damage the quality of the dialogue by forcing students who are underprepared and under-motivated to fully participate with their classmates. I notice this phenomenon most clearly in the late winter months just before spring, when students are feeling tired and numbed by the repetition of the school day and school activities. Some years I take a break from the circles for a few weeks to allow students to recharge their batteries and approach Socratic circles from a fresh point of view. Listening to student comments and attitudes toward the dialogue often reveals when a break is needed.

Selecting Text and Establishing Connections to Course Content

Most important in deciding when and how often Socratic circles should be used is determining how a particular piece of text and the dialogue it generates might expand students' learning of a particular idea, theme, or subject. Aligning particular Socratic circles with material students are currently learning is important for two reasons. First, it allows teachers to show that the strategy and the dialogue are helping students achieve the daily, unit, and course outcomes of the class. Second, students report that they find Socratic circles more enjoyable and meaningful when the dialogue relates to material being studied.

Teachers must carefully choose text that expands upon a theme the class has been exploring, contradicts a position or stand that helps to illuminate a larger issue, or helps students make sense of the world around them. For example, I have had great success in using the lyrics to Johnny Cash's "Man in Black" after discussing the character of Atticus Finch in *To Kill a Mockingbird*, and in partnering the myth of 1930s blues guitarist Robert Johnson with the Faust theme in literature. These selections expand students' understanding of the theme and help them draw connections between popular culture and literary elements. Selecting text at random, or selecting text that cannot be connected to the curriculum of the class, only works against the process we seek to instill in our students. For Socratic Circles to be successful, teachers must select text that is relevant to the current curriculum, insightful, thought-provoking, and relevant to students' lives.

Good "text," then, comes from a wide range of sources, many of which are not even text in the traditional sense of the word. Poetry, short fiction, long fiction, nonfiction, drama, news stories, speeches, articles, letters, journals, lyrics, diaries, e-mail notes, advertisements, reviews, greeting cards, comic strips—the list is almost endless. However, there are just as many nontext selections that work equally well (and sometimes work even better): paintings, sculpture, musical compositions, billboards, television and video clips, films, photographs, and murals, just to name a few. Selections of text are limited only by the imaginations of those involved.

Regardless of the genre, form, or medium, however, all chosen pieces of text should possess some basic characteristics. The text should be something students can relate to and identify with, something that is relevant to their own lives or their own learning. Entirely abstract or random text that has no relevance to students contradicts the process of the Socratic circle. To build collaborative understanding through cooperative inquiry students must be able to see purpose and value in the text they are discussing. The text should also be thought-provoking and examine a concept or idea in a philosophical manner that allows them to use the higher-order thinking skills of analysis, synthesis, and evaluation. Good text raises questions in the minds of students, and these questions become the basis of dialogue.

Finally, good text should tie in with the theme or content of the curriculum currently being taught and explored in class. Texts selected at random or on a whim may produce excellent dialogue, but that dialogue is less productive if it does not help students expand the learning that is already taking place in class. Exceptions to this sometimes exist early in the process of teaching students how to engage in Socratic circles. In fact one of my most successful Socratic circles, one that spurs a tremendous level of critical thinking and student engagement, is based on a painting that was discovered hidden away in a storage closet in our high school art department. Ironically, no one remembers who painted the work or when it was completed, but it continues to capture student imagination and create excellent dialogue. The painting, shown in Figure 7.1, appears to contain several symbolic elements, such as the words "I lie" within the woman's lips and the missing eyes of the figure in the foreground, that lead most students to explore the "blindness" of teenage relationships and their record of frequent failure. Although the discovered painting does not align with the required curriculum of any of my classes, it serves perfectly to demonstrate for students the power of mutual inquiry and the collaborative building of understanding and meaning.

Figure 7.1
Student painting

Finding good text for a Socratic circle can at times be amazingly simple and at other times be amazingly frustrating. Searching for a piece of text can be a bit like looking for a needle in a haystack. With the wide range of possibilities out there, selecting one piece of text to spur dialogue can be intimidating. Bearing in mind the three selection criteria—relevance to students, springboard for philosophical thought, and curricular connectedness—there are a number of places where teachers can look for help. Classic literature is a cornucopia of reading that can arouse student curiosity and philosophical questions. The Great Books Foundation <www.greatbooks.org> and Junior Great Books are a fantastic place to start. Likewise, readings from The Touchstones Discussion Group <www.touchstones.org> are specifically selected for Socratic circle–like discussions. A good literature anthology or literary concordance can also serve as a warehouse for excellent selections of text. Supplemental materials included with textbooks are often an untapped resource. I use many of the art transparencies and reading selections from standardized assessments as Socratic circle texts.

Library media specialists are indispensable resources when it comes to searching for text. They know what is contained in their collections far better than we could ever know, they know where materials in their collections are, often better than they know the backs of their hands, and most of the time, they absolutely love to see the materials they have purchased, catalogued, and stored finally put to use. If you ask, many media specialists will even keep an eye out for new materials that may come along as well, especially if they know the specific themes you are hoping to have your students explore.

Many reference works within the library are also great resources. Whether about art, music, literature, history, biography, or something else, selections of text can be found on almost every page. One of my favorite resources is the *Green Book of Songs by Subject: The Thematic Guide to Popular Music.* This book contains references to more than 35,000 different songs from a variety of genres, organized into 1,800 thematic categories. I have supplemented entire units with songs listed in this book and have helped students build many successful dialogues around the wealth contained within its pages. Another excellent resource is *The Reading Teacher's Book of Lists*, which provides 190 lists for developing instructional materials and lesson planning. The Internet is also a quick and easy reference for lists of works that can be thematically linked to the curriculum. A simple keyword on a search engine can often produce far more possibilities than a teacher has time to wade through.

Fortunately, seeking out good text for a Socratic circle grows easier with time. Once the three criteria for selecting text become a habit of mind and a habit of perception, our brains learn to identify good text quickly. The world seems to open up and a teacher can find multiple selections of text on a daily basis, without even trying. In the back of my lesson plan book, I keep an ongoing list of ideas for Socratic circle texts. I simply jot down the title of the piece and a reference to the connection I see to the curriculum of my classes. This list serves as another warehouse of potential ideas.

Perhaps the greatest of all sources for texts is our students. Some of the very best Socratic circles I have ever led have been based on text that was originally suggested to me by a student. A simple question such as, Can anyone think of a piece of text that would fit in well with our study of *Romeo and Juliet*? can produce answers and possibilities that I would never have come up with. The teacher still needs to weigh these selections carefully to see if they stimulate philosophical questions and are suitable. But when generating a list of possibilities, students can be a phenomenal asset.

Cross-Curricular Opportunities

Another important use of Socratic circles within the curriculum is in creating cross-curricular learning opportunities that tie material and objectives from multiple classes together into one dialogue. These opportunities allow students to process ideas on an entirely different level, make connections among content areas, and establish a greater sense of relevance for that learning to their own lives. In many ways, any Socratic circle can be a cross-curricular learning situation because so much of the background knowledge and information students bring to a dialogue is from their learning in other classes. As Adler (1982) suggested with his Three Columns of Learning, the Column One content of multiple classes and the Column Two skills of multiple classes can come together and be interwoven into the dialogue that is created. However, purposefully using Socratic circles to draw out ideas from other classes and make connections between courses can motivate and stimulate increased student learning.

Whether teachers are team teaching courses or working closely with teachers from other content areas or are simply familiar with what is being studied in other classes as it is reported by students, using Socratic circles to tap into those cross-curricular resources can be very effective. For example, with my high school juniors enrolled in an American literature class, I collaborate with our junior-level American history teachers when they reach the Revolutionary period to teach a thematic unit on the characteristics of American identity. Although we do not team-teach in the sense of combining classes and teaching in the same room, there is a great amount of interaction between what we are doing in English class and what students are doing in history class. After studying such works as the Declaration of Independence and Patrick Henry's "Speech in the Virginia Convention" in history class and discussing the characteristics that defined the colonists' emerging sense of national identity, we might use the Gettysburg Address, selections from Thoreau's "Civil Disobedience," selections from King's "Letter from Birmingham Jail," or even selections from President George W. Bush's address to Congress after the September 11 terrorist attacks in English class to explore how these ideas and characteristics have changed or not changed over time. By combining our efforts in such a manner, students expand their understanding of the historical relevance of the ideas that shaped the American Revolution and can examine the persuasive strategies and modeling that occurred as these writers formed their arguments around common motifs and used similar techniques to accomplish their goals.

After such cross-curricular opportunities teachers have seen improved test scores and more insightful and thorough student essays. Socratic circles and the integration of content and skills that they provide create powerful opportunities for students to expand their learning beyond the objectives of a particular unit or particular course and create the very type of learning that Adler (1982) argues is too often missing from public education.

One example of such a cross-curricular opportunity is establishing a connection between visual art and the study of Shakespeare's *Julius Caesar.* I modeled this practice after an activity in an undergraduate class titled Teaching Reading in the Content Area, in which artwork from the collections of the Spencer Museum of Art at the University of Kansas were integrated into our coursework (Barry 1997). After reading the play, we hold a Socratic circle about the art displayed in Figure 7.2.

Students are able to draw on their learning from reading the play and discuss their perceptions of the "story" told through the art. This activity has served as an excellent review as students sift through the details of the play and weigh the moral and ethical questions of the conspiracy, better preparing them for either a test or an analytical essay on the work.

The dialogue inspired by John Buck's *Aloha* always proves to be one of the most challenging discussions for students each year but also one of the most rewarding. Some students go so far as to research the historical details of Caesar's life that do not appear in Shakespeare's play in order to better understand the symbolic elements of the artwork.

High-Stakes Testing

Although the type of constructivist learning that Socratic circles embody and the student empowerment they create are powerful entities in our pedagogy, the forces of public education sometimes disagree with this approach and its relevance to our mission. Reality tells us that teachers have less and less time to cover a body of curricular content that grows larger and larger with each passing school year. In light of increased calls for accountability and standardized testing, teachers are feeling more and

FIGURE 7.2 John
Buck's *Aloha*

more pressure to not only cover the "right" content but also to create students who can produce the "right" answers on such tests. Many teachers, when faced with these daunting pressures, have turned to the strategies that are the most time efficient, namely the drill-and-recitation, teacher-centered strategies of lecture, worksheets, multiple-choice quizzes, and so on.

And in an era of high-stakes testing and Annual Yearly Progress reports, these goals become even more important. When asked how schools and teachers could deal with the pressure of high-stakes testing, Heidi Hayes Jacobs, an educational consultant and curriculum expert, says reading skills are crucial:

> *The one subset of skills that's requisite for any test or any assessment is literacy. Every test these kids take entails reading. Schools can't lose when they help students become more discriminating and discerning readers; more critical responders in their writing; and more effective speakers, reflective listeners, and active note-takers. (Perkins-Gough 2003, p. 18)*

Because Socratic circles ask students to read critically, probing beneath the surface meaning and exploring relevance to larger personal and social meaning, they help build and reinforce essential skills students must master for standardized tests. The skills of critical thinking and problem solving are also reinforced as students engage in dialogue and seek both meaning and understanding.

CONCLUSION

Some might view Socratic circles as an unnecessary and ineffective manner in which to teach content, but when carefully planned and aligned with the curriculum, they can be powerful learning opportunities that help students expand their understanding of multiple content areas, further develop life skills, and better prepare for the rigors of high-stakes testing. And although our curricula are already overflowing with enough standards and benchmarks to keep us busy for far longer than our course schedules allow, there are ways to incorporate Socratic circles into our practice without sacrificing other content. The strategy embodies the type of real-world situations of Adler's Column Three and provides students the cross-curricular and personal connections that can greatly expand the depth of their learning.

Chapter 8

ASSESSMENT AND FOLLOW-UP ACTIVITIES

DIALOGUE INSPIRED BY A. E. HOUSMAN'S "TO AN ATHLETE DYING YOUNG."

COPELAND: *Can anyone connect the content of this poem with what we do every week in our Socratic circles?*

LACY: *They're exactly the same. Both deal with having potential and making sure that that potential is realized, not only in the mind of the central figure but in the mind of the people watching as well.*

CHRISTINA: *I don't get it. What do you mean?*

LACY: *Well, like it says right here, "From fields where glory does not stay." Every week we've had these Socratic circles, and every week we've been the ones to have to work and struggle to figure out what this means. No one else can do it for us. We've got this way of figuring out what things mean and why they are important, but if we don't work for it, nothing happens. It's just like in the poem. This athlete dying young doesn't realize how good he has it. He's going to die as a champion and not have to struggle with life after his fifteen minutes of fame.*

CODY: *So, you're saying that whatever meaning or interpretation we find in this poem is worthless because the world isn't going to respect it?*

LACY: *No, what I'm saying is that whatever meaning or interpretation we find in this poem is only as good as what we go out and do with it. We can't be content to just sit here*

123

and say, "Wow, cool poem" and go on with our lives. Now that we've figured this thing out, we have to find ways to remember it and make sure we live it.

BRAD: *So, if we don't remember it, we're going to die?*

LACY: *Not literally, but yes, we'll live lives that aren't as full and rich as they could be.*

CHRISTINA: *But I still don't get it. How is this poem just like our Socratic circles every week?*

LACY: *Because this is what our Socratic circles do for us. They teach us a way to approach our lives, not only our reading and our writing and all that school stuff, but we can look at and talk about anything and figure out why it is important and how it affects us.*

STEPHANIE: *No, I see what she means. Socratic circles teach us to appreciate the abilities we have and appreciate the world around us, regardless of what others may say. That's the fifteen minutes of fame thing. Sure, if we tell a group of our friends that we read this poem today and it changed our lives, they're going to laugh at us and tell us we're nuts. But we're all in here right now, and we've all just figured this thing out together. Whether the world agrees with us or even remembers what we've talked about isn't important; what's important is that we remember.*

LACY: *It's like the end of the poem. "And round that early-laurelled head / Will flock to gaze the strengthless dead." Not everyone will care about what we come up with for a meaning; the world isn't going to stop and suddenly start paying attention to everything we think and say, but there will be those who agree with us, those that at least in spirit will applaud what we've done and what we've come up with.*

STEPHANIE: *And it's our job to make sure we live up to what we discover. It's our job to make sure that we never forget, even if the rest of the world does.*

LACY: *Exactly.*

The final role of the teacher in a Socratic circle involves assessing student performance and creating follow-up activities and assignments to extend the learning. Not only is assessment important in terms of documenting student success and achievement, but it also helps in driving student reflection and creating goals to guide future learning. Effective assessment of Socratic circle performance involves multiple strategies, both formal and informal, and involves honest and forthright discussion among students about success and areas for improvement.

Creating follow-up activities for students after the dialogue is one way to enhance learning and keep the ideas and lessons gained foremost in their minds. Follow-up activities also serve an important role in guiding students' minds back to the content- and skills-based curricula of the class and strengthen the connections made between the text and the other class material being learned.

ASSESSMENT

Assessment can take many forms during a Socratic circle. Obviously, the comments provided by the outside circle offer students immediate feedback on their performance. The Socratic Circle Feedback Form in the Appendix allows some of these comments to be recorded. Likewise, if the teacher engages in the role of note taker, scorekeeper, or mapmaker, this information can also be shared during the reflection and feedback period. Students in the outside circle can even be assigned the role of scorekeeper or mapmaker before the conversation begins to provide multiple opinions and free the teacher to complete more formal types of assessments.

Assessment can also take many forms after a Socratic circle. Scorecards and maps can be tracked over time to show improvement. Teachers can use rubrics to assess in a more formal manner the performance of either the circles or individual students. Finally, students can engage in various reflective writings to document their opinions of how the dialogue went.

Informal Assessment of the Inner Circle

One of the most important types of assessment that can occur within Socratic circles is the informal assessment of student performance both by the teacher and by the students themselves. The role of the outer circle in making observations and providing feedback, as explained in Chapter 5, is crucial to the Socratic circle process. Not only do students in the inner circle receive instant feedback on their performance, but the comments help students establish goals to drive future learning and reinforce the process of continuous growth.

Although this type of informal feedback is probably most important in student minds, the teacher can provide other types of informal assessment that can guide students and the Socratic circle process itself. I complete three primary types of informal assessment as I observe the dialogue in my room: note taking, scorekeeping, and mapmaking. Each of these strategies has its strengths and drawbacks, but unfortunately only one can be used at a time while observing the dialogue of the inner circle. Once students are familiar with the process of Socratic circles and understand what I do in each of these three roles, I sometimes ask someone in the outer circle to perform one of the roles as well, thereby expanding the amount and quality of informal assessment taking place.

NOTE TAKER

One of the most productive strategies for informally assessing the dialogue of the inner circle is taking notes. This allows the teacher to keep an anecdotal record of the content and behavior of the inner circle on paper so that it can be reviewed later. I do this by creating a simple two-column chart. On the left side, I record the content of the conversation taking place, noting subtopics discussed, important questions, and references to the text. In the right-hand column, I note two types of information. Much like the outer-circle members, I note the behavior of the inner circle, jotting down observations of participation, leadership, and off-task activity. And I keep a running list of the strategies the inner circle uses to begin to unlock the meaning presented in the text. For instance, students may discuss symbolism, the repetition of words or ideas, the use of punctuation, the importance of the title, the writer's tone, or other elements.

This strategy has several strengths that help improve the overall quality of the dialogue. Having a tangible record of what was discussed and how the discussion progressed can be invaluable. Many students who are absent on the day of a Socratic circle will read over the two-column notes to get a sense of the discussion. This is particularly helpful when Socratic circles begin to draw ideas from previous dialogues and reach higher and higher levels of thinking. These notes can help students review or catch up on what was missed. The record of student behavior within a Socratic circle can also be useful to teachers. Having documentation to show specific dates and contexts in which a student behaved, either positively or negatively, can be helpful in parent-teacher conferences, Individualized Education Plan meetings, and in helping to provide remediation to students struggling with the Socratic circle process. Documenting the dialogues that occur in a qualitative manner can be valuable for a wide range of reasons.

The amount of time it takes to complete these notes, however, can limit the teacher's ability to fill other roles during the activity. At times, I have difficulty simply keeping up with both columns of notes and tracking both the content and the behavior of the discussion. To then add participation as needed in the inner circle and monitoring the outer circle, the teacher can quickly become overwhelmed. As students are learning the process early in the school year, I typically avoid this assessment technique because of the time it takes to complete. After students have participated in three or four Socratic circles and are more comfortable and confident in their performance, I am able to begin taking notes with more success. A final weakness of this technique is that the notes themselves represent the dialogue from only one observer's point of view. Socratic circles welcome multiple points of view, but the notes themselves can be biased toward one perspective or another. Although I do my best to record the conversation in as an objective manner as possible, some students disagree with what I record as the main ideas of a particular dialogue.

Because of the time that taking notes requires and the fact that different observers see the dialogue in different lights, I have had multiple students in the outer circle fulfill the role of note taker. This allows multiple points of view to emerge in regard to the conversation and releases the teacher to participate more in the other elements of the dialogue. Great benefit can be reaped from having students then review and compare the multiple sets of notes that were recorded, often leading to insightful conversations that expand and improve the meaning found by the inner circle. Although note taking is by far the most time and attention consuming of the informal assessments, the information it produces can be quite valuable to students and teachers alike.

SCOREKEEPER

A far easier manner in which to record information about the dialogue of the inner circle is to keep score. Although Socratic circles do not pit students against one another to come up with the best questions or the most insightful ideas, some students are motivated by competition and participate more fully when competitive elements are added to the activity. The information provided by this strategy can help provide those elements.

At the beginning of each inner circle's dialogue, I jot down the name of each student. As the conversation begins, I add tally marks next to each student's name or initials each time he or she contributes to the dialogue. Whereas a student might earn one tally for contributing basic information, I might award two to a student who poses a question to the circle or refers to the text in his or her contribution, or three to a student who provides a particularly insightful response to a question. In this manner, students earn tallies not only for the number of times they participate in the dialogue but also for the quality of the contributions they make. Figure 8.1 represents what a completed scorecard might look like.

After the conversation I can quickly total the tallies for each student and report to the inner circle how each person performed. I am careful to always refer to these as "tallies" and not as "points" to reduce the confusion between these records and the records that might eventually appear in the gradebook. Students then are able to contemplate in their own minds how they fared in comparison with the other members of the inner circle. For some students this type of competition provides reinforcement for the process and a sense of accomplishment for a job well done. For other students the tallies are completely insignificant. A modification of this idea includes using simple tally marks and question marks to distin-

FIGURE 8.1
Scorekeeper tally
sheet

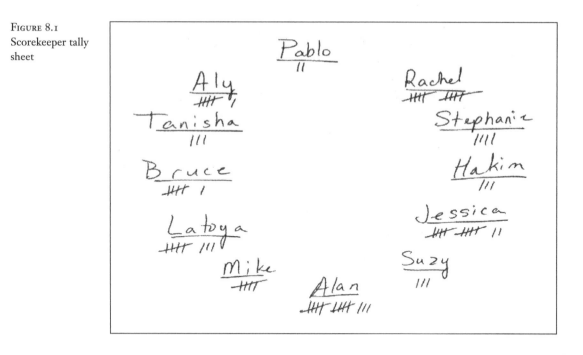

guish between the types of comments made within the dialogue. For example, it can be reported that a student accumulated fourteen tallies and asked six questions. This can be valuable in helping students see the importance of asking questions within the circle and in determining which students pose the greatest number of questions to the group.

Scorekeeping is a very quick and almost effortless way to generate simple information that can be reported to the inner circle and help them reflect and establish goals for future Socratic circles. Because scorekeeping provides quantitative information, students can quickly self-assess and make individual comparisons among their performance, the performances of their peers, and their own past performances, giving them immediate feedback. Over time students can even be asked to track or graph their tallies, demonstrating their growth through participation in Socratic circles.

This method of assessment, however, has its limitations. The overall quality of feedback provided is not as comprehensive as the anecdotal note-taker records, and it provides no information about the quality of a student's individual contributions. The performance of each student is simply boiled down to a number. And although some students find these numbers helpful in judging their own performance and adding elements of competition to the process, numbers can negatively affect the overall quality of dialogue when students become more focused on accumulating tallies than on building meaningful dialogue.

The scorekeeping method of informal assessment can help students reflect, and it gives them immediate feedback on their performance in the inner circle. Like note taking, this is not a strategy I use with every Socratic circle; I find it more useful to use occasionally to graphically represent the dialogue.

MAPMAKING

A third informal assessment technique that also produces a graphic representation of the inner circle's dialogue is mapmaking. Whereas the scorekeeper tracks the individual performances of students in the inner circle, the mapmaker documents their interactions as a whole group, tracing the flow of the conversation from one person to another. This information helps the inner circle examine their dialogue after it is complete, focusing their attention on details often overlooked while engaged in the dialogue itself, and can help expose both positive and negative patterns of behavior.

To make a map, I jot down the names of students in the inner circle in relation to where they are seated, just as I do in the role of scorekeeper. However, when the dialogue begins, I place the point of the pencil next to the name of the first person who speaks and don't lift the pencil point until the dialogue is complete. In this manner I trace the conversation from person to person, creating a map of the discussion. Figure 8.2 represents what a completed map might look like.

By far the least time and attention consuming of the three informal assessments described here, mapmaking can help students identify some of the specific behaviors that affect their dialogue. For example, when a question is posed by one student and another student answers that question, an interesting dynamic is created in which these two students begin to direct their comments to each other, to the exclusion of other members of the group. And although they may be completely unaware of this at the time, the results will be clearly documented in the map, represented by an abundance of lines between their two names. Likewise, if students have grown accustomed to directing their comments and contributions to certain members of the circle or to students sitting in certain positions within the circle to the exclusion of others, this, too, can be documented. Having evidence of such dynamics can help students explore their antecedents and better understand why they occur. If necessary, students can then brainstorm strategies to alter their behaviors and improve their dialogue. Comparing these maps over time can also help students see their growth. Typically, maps made early in the process of Socratic circles at the beginning of the year show lines of participation among only a few students. As time passes and students develop stronger skills in dialogue, the lines are distributed more evenly, revealing more balanced participation.

FIGURE 8.2
Mapmaker example

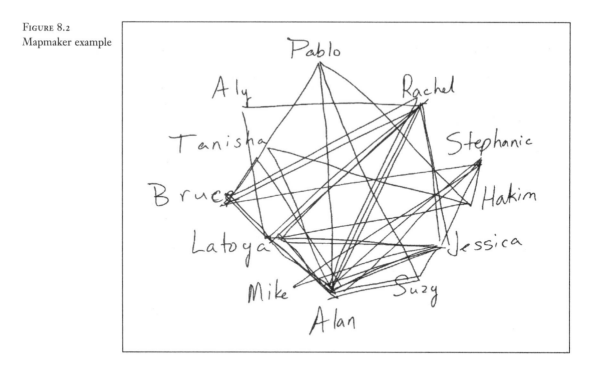

Perhaps the greatest limitation in this informal method of assessment is that there is no information about the context in which the flow of conversation occurs. For example, there is no difference in appearance between a map that shows students' natural interaction and one that shows a more premeditated conversation in which one student is directing comments to others, perhaps by posing a question to a specific student. In both cases, a line is drawn to show the movement of participation between students, but the context of that movement is unclear. Like the scorecard, the map reveals no information about the individual exchanges between students but rather shows the movements of the group's conversation as a whole.

The ease of the mapmaker's role makes it a tempting option when choosing an informal assessment strategy because it can be completed with very little thought or energy. However, I find it the least helpful of the three strategies. In the first few Socratic circles I use it because it shows students the details of their performance and helps to focus their attention on improving as a group. And with practice in completing Socratic circles, students in the outer circle generally note and offer feedback on some of the same details shown in the mapmaker's chart. Therefore, I usually abandon mapmaking after the first few initial Socratic circles. However, it is also one of the easiest assessment methods to teach to students. Typically after seeing me make a map once, students understand the method and can assume the role on their own, leaving me free to fill other roles. If, however, I see a need or weakness in the behaviors of the inner circle that could be addressed with mapmaking, I return to the strategy as needed.

The real benefit in all three of these informal assessment strategies is in using them within the discussion of the outer circle. Rather than commenting on what I notice in the scorecards, maps, and anecdotal notes, I generally use a line of Socratic questioning with the outer circle to generate insight into what they reveal. Again, students generally take to heart the comments of their peers more than those of their teacher, and in this way, the assessments are more effective in influencing the overall quality of dialogue.

Formal Assessment of the Inner Circle

Whereas informal assessments greatly assist students in improving their dialogue skills and provide cursory information for outside observers, formal assessment can provide a much more structured and measurable analysis of student growth. I have found the most productive formal assessment to be the use of a rubric to gauge student performance in Socratic circles. Figure 8.3 represents the rubric that I have developed to assess and track my students' growth over time.

The eight criteria listed across the top of the rubric are skills that I have found to be crucial to Socratic circle success. Students who demonstrate these skills typically are able to create meaningful and insightful dialogue on a consistent basis. The criteria represent a wide range of skills and behaviors: preparing for discussion of the text with close analytical reading and annotations, referring to the text within the dialogue, maintaining focus and engagement in the dialogue, encouraging others, effective listening and questioning, presenting ideas in a civil manner, and being open to multiple points of view on a given topic or selection of text.

The rubric is rather large and can be cumbersome at first, but with experience I have found it to be a fast, easy, and reliable way to evaluate student performance. Most of the time the rubric itself is not visible during the dialogue. I spend one class period early in the process explaining the rubric to students and discussing the importance of the eight criteria and how each can positively or adversely affect the quality of dialogue that occurs. We also discuss what behaviors we might see that would represent a particular numeric rating for different criteria, and occasionally role-play scripted situations and discuss how we would rate particular behaviors. Once students understand the rubric and the manner in which they are being evaluated, they grow comfortable with the process and the rubric itself slips from the foreground of their minds.

Student: _____   Hour: _____   Date: _____   Topic: _____

Socratic Circle Rubric	Reading of text and preparation for circle.	Engaged in discussion and stays on-task.	Supports ideas with references to the text.	Encourages thinking and participation in others.	Listens respectfully and builds from ideas of others.	Presents self and ideas in a civil and proper manner.	Questions insightfully and uses sound reasoning.	Accepts more than one point of view on the text.
5 Outstanding	Remarks and written work reveal a close, critical reading of the text and thorough preparation.	Demonstrates active and eager participation throughout entire circle. Keeps group on-task.	Makes specific references to text to support and defend ideas on a consistent basis.	Guides the direction and success of the circle and takes steps to involve all participants.	Listens unusually well. Comments indicate very accurate and perceptive listening.	Demonstrates respect and enthusiasm. Works to support all participants at all times.	Questions and ideas are apt, insightful, and logical; and contribute to construction of meaning.	Accepts points of view other than own and uses them to expand ideas and discover new meaning.
4 Good	Remarks and written work reveal a close, critical reading of the text, but preparation appears incomplete.	Active and eager participation in more than 80% of circle. Keeps self on-task always and others at times.	Makes specific references to text to support and defend ideas often and when challenged.	Attempts to guide circle and draw in participants and is most often successful.	Listens well. Pays attention and generally responds well to ideas and questions from others.	Demonstrates respect and enthusiasm. Supports all participants most of the time.	Questions and ideas are apt, insightful, and logical but may not fully help meaning construction.	Accepts points of view other than own and attempts to use them to discover new meaning.
3 Average	Remarks and written work reveal a close reading of the text, but ideas seem to be less than complete.	Active and eager participation in more than 50% of circle. Stays on-task most of the time.	Makes specific references to text to support and defend ideas only when challenged.	Attempts to guide circle and draw in participants but is not always effective.	Generally listens well but is not always attentive as evident in responses or body language.	Demonstrates respect but may be less than totally supportive of others at times.	Questions and comments are apt and logical but lack insight to move group forward.	Acknowledges other points of view but struggles to use them to expand meaning.
2 Below Average	Remarks and written work do not reveal a close, critical reading of the text.	Some active participation in circle; may be less than eager. Off-task frequently.	Makes few references to text to support and defend ideas even when challenged.	Attempts to guide circle and draw in reluctant participants are not successful.	Comments tend to reflect an earlier failure to listen carefully to what was said.	Speech and manner suggest lack of understanding of purpose. Lacks sense of teamwork.	Questions and ideas reveal personal reactions, but not logical, apt arguments.	Argues with other points of view and reluctantly acknowledges them as a possibility.
1 Not Acceptable	Remarks and written work suggest the text was not read.	No active participation in circle. Others may be distracted by behavior.	Makes no specific references to text to support and defend ideas.	Makes no attempts to guide circle or draw in reluctant participants.	Does not listen adequately. Comments or body language suggestive of inattentiveness.	Does not display respect or enthusiasm for circle or other participants.	Remarks are illogical, difficult to follow, and offer the group no benefit.	Does not acknowledge or accept other points of view.

FIGURE 8.3 Socratic Circle Rubric

During our Socratic circles I typically use the scorecard to record my ratings of individual student performance (see Figure 8.4). I have found this incredibly helpful in managing the use of the rubric. While students are engaged in dialogue, I can record simple judgments of specific behaviors in the appropriate column and row. For example, if a particular student asks an insightful question, I can place a small plus sign in the appropriate box, or if a student speaks to the group with a less-than-respectful attitude, I might write a small minus sign. After the dialogue is complete, I can review the marks and assign each student a numeric rating for each of the eight criteria. These scorecards and the ratings they report can be tracked over time, showing student growth and development in these eight areas.

As with the informal assessments, I do not use the rubric and scorecard with every Socratic circle; however, I do try to use them on a regular basis. And unlike the informal assessments, which require my time and attention during the dialogue, I can rate students with accuracy and efficiency even after a dialogue is completed, whether between classes, during lunch, or even after school. In this way I can include both formal and informal assessments of the same Socratic circle to create a more accurate and descriptive evaluative picture of the dialogue that took place.

Typically, I keep all the various assessments of the inner circle together on a clipboard for each class, making sure each assessment includes the date of the dialogue and the title of the text being discussed. In this way, I can track student growth over time and review relevant information about particular students and the class as a whole, and make changes to the way we engage in Socratic circles. This information and evaluation is important in improving the process and quality of student dialogue. This information can also be discussed with parents and administrators and be used to paint a picture of student behavior and performance in class. Many students even ask to review their performance over time to gauge their own growth as well.

Assessment of the Outer Circle

Like the inner circle, the outer circle can be assessed using both formal and informal methods. However, because the role of the outer circle is to provide feedback and help to evaluate the performance of the inner circle, I assess the outer circle far less often and in less detail to keep student attention focused on improving the quality of the inner circle's dialogue.

Informal assessment of the outer circle can be done quite easily by having students turn in a brief summary of the observations and feedback they offer the inner circle. When using the feedback form (see Appendix), I have students turn them in after the Socratic circle so I can monitor the

Socratic Circle Scorecard

5 = Outstanding   4 = Good   3 = Average   2 = Below Average   1 = Not Acceptable

Class: _____   Hour: _____   Date: _____   Topic: _____

Student's Name (Initials)	Reading of text and preparation for circle.	Engaged in discussion and stays on-task.	Supports ideas with references to the text.	Encourages thinking and participation in others.	Listens respectfully and builds from ideas of others.	Presents self and ideas in a civil and proper manner.	Questions insightfully and uses sound reasoning.	Accepts more than one point of view on the text.
1.								
2.								
3.								
4.								
5.								
6.								
7.								
8.								
9.								
10.								
11.								
12.								
13.								
14.								
15.								

First Inner Circle   Second Inner Circle   Time in Discussion: _____ minutes

FIGURE 8.4 Socratic Circle Scorecard

evaluating they are doing. When not using the form, I occasionally have students in the outer circle turn in a simple two-column chart that lists what the inner circle did well in their dialogue and areas in which they could improve. Over time these summaries can show how student thinking has grown in offering constructive feedback to the inner circle and how their minds and attitudes toward the qualities that make for effective dialogue grow and change as well.

Another form of informal assessment (and a beneficial follow-up activity to a Socratic circle) is to ask students to briefly explain in writing how the feedback of the outer circle helped them individually evaluate their performance in dialogue. These anecdotal records offer multiple points of view on the feedback offered, and I am always interested to see how students interpret and respond to the feedback given. Asking students to do this in writing allows them to vent their frustration with some of the feedback they have received (often a productive endeavor) privately and can help the teacher identify areas of individual student interactions that may need to be addressed.

I have also enjoyed success in having willing students share with the class some of their responses to feedback after it has been written. Hearing some of their own thoughts and attitudes echoed by their peers reinforces the legitimacy of their thinking and can help students feel more satisfied with the process of offering feedback. This activity also offers an opportunity to praise those students who offer insightful and constructive feedback and offers other students model examples of such feedback. This short activity can be done in only a few minutes and can add closure to the end of a class period. It is also an excellent way to refocus student minds at the beginning of the next class period.

More formal assessment of the outer circle could be done with the use of a rubric similar to the one used for the inner circle. The criteria for such a rubric might include the civility with which the feedback was offered, the feedback being offered in a constructive manner, and the overall quality and depth of the feedback. Although formal assessment of the outer circle could be done quickly and easily, I have resisted it in my classes. Having students offer constructive criticism of their peers is often an adjustment for students in itself, and evaluating them on that feedback can inhibit them from growing more comfortable with the process. I have found informal assessment of the outer circle to be sufficient.

Assigning Grades for Socratic Circles

With all of the various forms of assessment, there is ample opportunity and information to assign grades for Socratic circles, if a teacher so desires. Dialogue, however, is a verbal form of collaborative thinking, brainstorming, and exploring ideas, similar to the prewriting stage of composition. Although we may ask students to complete and turn in prewriting of some kind with a writing assignment, we rarely grade it for its quality and insightfulness; we assume that quality and insight will carry over and be revealed in the writing assignment itself. Likewise, good dialogue reveals itself in the assignments and activities that follow Socratic circles. Whether in essays, on exams, or in other forms of classroom discussion, the results of classroom dialogue manifest themselves on their own and influence the grades students earn on multiple other assignments.

With this idea in mind, I resist assigning grades for the dialogue and the Socratic circles themselves, and prefer to assign grades for the assignments and activities that come both before and after the discussion. Because the dialogue is student generated, student controlled, and student driven, assigning a grade to it can stigmatize students and be counterproductive to the continuous growth process. Students can become more concerned with the grade earned for the Socratic circle than they are with the process. Other teachers prefer to assign grades for the Socratic circles themselves, sometimes translating tallies or rubric ratings into points in the gradebook.

In my classes I assign grades to the students' annotations of the text to hold them accountable for adequately preparing for the dialogue within a Socratic circle in much the same manner that a teacher might assign grades for a reading quiz on a particular novel or other literary work. Although these grades are minor in the larger scope of the overall class, they reinforce to students that preparation is necessary to produce high-quality, insightful dialogue. Because dialogue and annotations involve student reactions, comments, and questions much more so than factual correctness, the grades are assigned as much on quantity of annotations as on quality. Students have no way of knowing the given direction or content of a classroom dialogue and therefore must prepare for a broad range of possible topics. Of course, I am always looking for comments and questions that reveal critical thought and insight as well. In this way annotations can be graded quickly by simply skimming the comments and questions written on the text.

FOLLOW-UP ACTIVITIES

Because Socratic circles allow students to work with content previously learned and to further develop learning skills, they can synthesize the curriculum and expand student growth. However, the classroom dialogue created by Socratic circles can also serve as a springboard into additional activities and learning opportunities. Because student dialogue is a generative process that helps students construct meaning and understanding, assignments and activities can be created for students to develop those ideas more formally both as individuals and as members of a group.

Reflective Writing

One of the easiest follow-up activities for students to complete after a discussion is engaging in reflective writing about what they learned through the dialogue. This reflective writing can be done in any number of ways that might vary depending on teachers, classes, formats, and time constraints. Some teachers prefer to have students keep a journal of their participation in Socratic circles. Each entry comments on the content created in the dialogue, the student's own performance, and his or her perception of the performance of peers. In having students keep journals, teachers have reported that student thought deepens and becomes more critical over time as they begin to draw connections among the various dialogues and trace themes and central ideas through the various pieces of text. I have even noticed that after a particular Socratic circle students will return to previous entries in their journals, expanding their writing to include new ideas and perspectives on the previous dialogue. Reflective journals are one way of encouraging students to believe that dialogue is an integral component of classroom instruction that helps bind together the other content and skills being learned. Figure 8.5 shows an example of a student's journal entry after a Socratic circle.

One of the clear benefits of these journals is that they do not need to be assessed by teachers after every Socratic circle. I have my students turn in their journals perhaps only once per grading period, only as a way of holding them accountable for keeping up with the assignments. The comments that I write on the journal entries are concise and focus on praising students for offering insight that was not shared during class and suggesting places where their entries might be expanded and their ideas made more clear. In this way the grading of student journals is as quick and easy as possible for the teacher, and the high level of student ownership of the journals is maintained.

Typically, I also have my students compile their journals over the course of the school year and complete a Socratic circle portfolio at the end. These portfolios include their annotations of the text selections, their reflective entries from their journals about the texts and the dialogues they created, and an introductory letter that explains the contents of the portfolio and allows the students to comment on their perceptions of their growth and learning through Socratic circles. These portfolios have been very successful in helping students see their own growth over time and see the power of Socratic circles and dialogue in their own learning.

FIGURE 8.5 Journal
Entry Example

For our Socratic circle yesterday we examined and discussed the poem "To an Athlete Dying Young" by A. E. Housman. After listening to the first group find a literal understanding, we decided to look for some symbolism and find an overall meaning. We decided that the poem wasn't necessarily related to an athlete, but to anyone living life. We came to the conclusion that the purpose of this piece was to show that it's important to live life in the moment because in the long run, it's more important what you get out of something than how you go about doing it. To come to this conclusion, my group took the poem one stanza at a time. We also identified connections between the piece and our own lives. After figuring out the meaning, we decided it related well to the process of Socratic circles. As long as you put forth effort and gain knowledge through the experience, it's not quite as important how you get there.

I personally felt like I contributed to our discussion. I was well prepared with question and ideas. I explained my idea of "15 minutes of fame" and how fame wouldn't last because society grows in fads. I said that you should be doing things for yourself, not for the benefits of others. Overall, our group was very balanced. Not one person took charge because so many people had opinions. Almost everyone actually spoke. Our main problem was preparation. The more we prepare, the more we have to talk about, which makes the circle run more smoothly.

After reading this poem the first couple of times, I still had no clue what it meant. My group was very helpful. There was an answer for all of my questions. I learned the opinions of others, and in this case, became stronger with my own. I've always known I should try my hardest in what I do, but this Socratic circle made me want to apply it. I don't think we realize how short life is and how much we take advantage of each and every day. I really do think I got something from this Socratic circle, and I enjoyed participating. I dug down below the surface meaning, and with the help of others, succeeded in finding an understanding I could grasp.

Reflective writing can also take the form of short reaction papers to individual Socratic circles. These writings can help students take the ideas and meanings explored in their dialogue and develop them in more formal, concrete terms. These papers have been successful in allowing students to share and include personal ideas that may not have been incorporated into the dialogue itself. This can greatly reduce the frustrations some students feel at being confined by the ideas and meaning created by the group. Students who believe differently than their peers appreciate the opportunity to document their own thinking and can feel validated by putting those thoughts in writing.

Regardless of the form of the writing, allowing students the opportunity to reflect upon and add to the student dialogue in a more personal and individual manner can be very productive. Often when students reexamine and review the dialogue, they see more deeply into the text and the ideas shared and are able to comment with more insight. A number of other follow-up activities can also be used with Socratic circles to expand the ideas and topics generated in student dialogue that can tap students' multiple intelligences and learning styles as well. Students can create artwork, musical compositions, dramatic performances, narratives, poems, persuasive pieces, reviews, letters to the class or to the author of the text, and so on to enhance their learning and document the growth that has taken place.

Creating Thesis Statements

Another follow-up activity I have had great success with is having students create a thesis statement for an imaginary literary essay on the text we have discussed. These thesis statements help students generalize the ideas explored in their dialogue and then boil the meaning down into a concise sentence. In addition to the value of having students generalize and summarize the discussion, I have seen tremendous value in terms of their growth in developing and writing clear, well-crafted thesis statements.

I teach students that a thesis statement for a literary analysis essay typically has three parts: a subject, a method, and a message. The subject portion identifies the author and title of the piece being written about, the method identifies the literary technique or device the author uses to convey meaning, and the message conveys the idea or lesson the author seeks to have the reader consider. Once students have been taught this basic framework, we begin by inserting these elements into a Mad-lib–style sentence as shown in Figure 8.6.

After several Socratic circles and several thesis statements, I encourage students to break away from the formulaic thesis statement and form their own sentences based on the content of what has been discussed. We continue to emphasize the inclusion of the subject, method, and message, but the thesis statements themselves grow into forms that are more individual for each student.

This activity greatly helps develop student skill in writing a thesis statement that is clear, specific, and descriptive of the ideas and argument the student might make in this imaginary essay. And because students are not focusing on the writing of the entire essay but are focused on one specific sentence, they are able to devote more of their attention and

FIGURE 8.6 Thesis Statement

In _____ , _____
        (title of piece)   (author's name)

employs _____ to reveal _____ .
              (method)   (message)

thought to the quality of the thesis statement. In a typical semester-long class, students might have the opportunity to construct only three or four thesis statements. By asking students to compose one for each of the dialogues they engage in, they get more practice writing thesis statements and their skill in this area is greatly improved.

Certainly teachers could have students write a more formal, analytical essay about a Socratic circle as well. Occasionally, as a semester final, I have students review the texts we have used for dialogue and select one to write about in an in-class essay. This assignment works particularly well when students have previously created a thesis statement and generated at least some reflective writing about the text. With these pieces in place, students are able to review prior thinking and writing and generate a new piece of writing of higher quality. Letting them choose which dialogue to base their writing on increases their opportunity to write about a topic they feel strongly about and think they can be successful with.

Socratic Circle Reflection

Another follow-up activity, and one that combines several elements of the above activities, is to ask students to complete the Socratic Circle Reflection assignment outlined in Figure 8.7. This assignment asks students not only to reflect upon the dialogue created and their performances in both the inner and outer circle, but also to document their growth with vocabulary and specific reading comprehension strategies.

This assignment has proved very successful in helping students extract the most from their Socratic circle experience. By focusing attention on specific content and specific skills and behaviors in each reflection, students are able to draw connections among the text, the curriculum of the class, their own experiences, and the outside world. In this manner, learning becomes relevant, important, and available for further study. By documenting and reflecting upon what took place, students not only process the information more clearly in their own minds but also have the information at their fingertips for future reference. Figure 8.8 represents an example of a student's Socratic Circle Reflection assignment.

Creating follow-up activities for Socratic circles can greatly enhance the overall quality of student growth and learning and provide additional assessment opportunities to judge the value and worth of student dialogue in the classroom. Whereas dialogue asks students to consider multiple points of view and multiple theories and interpretations of texts, ideas, and philosophies in a group setting, follow-up activities allow them to further process these thoughts and weigh them more carefully in their individual minds. Writing often enables students to evaluate those ideas more slowly and critically and can lead to a more formal expression of student thought.

Socratic Circle Reflection

Instructions

After each of our Socratic circles you will be responsible for turning in a two-page, single-spaced reflection on the experience. This reflection will comprise four sections: (1) vocabulary, (2) strategies/techniques for comprehension and analysis, (3) reflection on performance, and (4) reflection on content. The information below will help you understand what content needs to be placed in each of the four sections.

It is imperative that you keep these reflections in a safe place once they have been graded and returned. At the end of the semester they will be compiled into a portfolio and used as evidence to document your growth through Socratic circles. This portfolio will affect your final grade in this class. Not having each of the reflections on our circles will result in a lower grade. DO NOT LOSE THESE REFLECTIONS!!!

Also, because your final Socratic circle portfolio will ask you to show growth over time, it is in your best interest to make sure that you date each and every one of your Socratic circle reflections and identify the title of the text that served as the basis of discussion.

Vocabulary

In this section you will list *at least three words* from the selection of text that you either were unfamiliar with when you first read the piece or words that you felt your understanding of changed over the course of the Socratic circle itself. For each of the identified words you will need to list three additional pieces of information: (1) the part of speech for the word as it is used in the text, (2) a dictionary definition for the word as it is used in the context of the sentence, (3) two to three sentences describing how your understanding of the word developed and/or changed through the Socratic circle process.

example:
indivisible (adj)—incapable of undergoing division
The dictionary provided me with a basic understanding of this word, but it wasn't until we started discussing the text and the history of the Pledge of Allegiance that I truly began to understand the importance of this idea. After our discussion I realize that indivisibility is one goal of our country the Pledge tries to instill.

Strategies/Techniques for Comprehension and Analysis

In the section you will list *at least three strategies or techniques* that were used by either inner circle to comprehend and analyze the selection of text. *Strive to identify new strategies that were used for the first time.* For each identified strategy/technique listed, you will need to write a *2–3-sentence description* of how it was used.

example:
Use of metaphor—We discussed the scene the author described and how that was relevant to the meaning of the overall passage. Having the metaphor at the beginning of the piece helped the reader imagine the scene in his or her own mind and made understanding the author's main points much easier.

There are no right or wrong answers in this section, simply your opinions. This list of possible strategies/techniques could go on forever. However, this may be a type of thinking with which you are unfamiliar. In order to help you get started, here's a list of some other possible strategies:

Word choice	Use of repetition	Use of capitalization
Voice	Use of verb tense	Organization/Structure
Sentence structure	Use of punctuation	Author's attitude
Paraphrasing	Summarizing	

(continued on next page)

FIGURE 8.7 Socratic Circle Reflection

Reflection on Performance

This section will be divided into two paragraphs: (1) a description of how you performed as an individual in the Socratic circle and (2) a description of how your group performed in both the role of the inner circle and the role of the outer circle. Again, there are no right or wrong answers here, only well-expressed opinions. You *might* consider the following questions for each paragraph:

Individual Performance

- How would you rate your preparation for this Socratic circle? Why?
- How would you rate your contributions (both the number of times you spoke and the quality of what you said) to the conversation of the inner circle? Why?
- How would you rate the level of teamwork you displayed in the inner circle? Why?
- How would you rate the quality of feedback you gave while you were in the outer circle? Why?
- How could you personally have improved what transpired during the Socratic circle?
- What goals do you have for your next Socratic circle performance?

Group Performance

- How would you rate your group's preparation for this Socratic circle? Why?
- How would you rate the quality of the overall conversation of your inner circle? Why?
- How would you rate the level of teamwork displayed by your inner circle? Why?
- How would you rate the quality of feedback your group gave while in the outer circle? Why?

Reflection on Content

This final section will comprise three items: (1) a thesis statement for an "imaginary" essay you might write about the meaning and importance of the ideas expressed in the selection of text, (2) a paragraph in which you describe (in general terms) the main points you might make in that "imaginary" essay, and (3) a paragraph in which you make connections between the content of this selection of text and some element of your own experience. Elements you might consider connecting this text to include: what we are currently learning in this class, learning that has occurred in other classes, personal experiences from your life outside of school, experiences of friends and family members with which you are familiar, current events, movies, literature, music, art, etc. Like the previous three sections, this last paragraph has no right or wrong answers, only opinions.

Checklist

Before turning in a reflection, use the following checklist to ensure you have included all of the necessary requirements to receive full credit:

_____   Your name, the date of the Socratic circle, and the title of the selection of text

_____   Three vocabulary words, their parts of speech, appropriate definitions, and explanation

_____   Three techniques for comprehension and analysis with explanation

_____   One paragraph reflecting on your individual performance

_____   One paragraph reflecting on the performance of your group

_____   A thesis statement for an "imaginary" essay on this text

_____   One paragraph explaining the main points of that "imaginary" essay

_____   One paragraph explaining the connections you made between the text and your own life

FIGURE 8.7 Socratic Circle Reflection *(continued)*

Traveling Through the Dark
September 24, 2003

Vocabulary
Swerve—Verb—To turn aside or cause to turn aside from a straight line, course, etc.

This word used to mean to me in the sense of an object turning, a car, bike, or even your physical body. I guess I knew it could be used for mental and emotions as well but I never thought of it in that context. I took it for its literal meaning.

Heap—Noun—Many things lying together in a mass; pile; mound.

In the poem, Stafford used a noun that describes many things to describe a single animal. I think his use of the word was correct in making a point. As I think he meant even though it seemed like a single deer was there really an unborn fawn lay inside of it, meaning mistakes can affect more than one person or objects.

Through—Prep.—In one side and out the other side of; from end to end; between the parts of.

I guess it's sort of a subconscious thing to realize through means an end and beginning but rare, at least I didn't really ever think about it being much different than other prepositions. I think Stafford's use of it is not only witty but also very creative as it gets you thinking about the poem before you even read it.

Strategies
Symbolism—Both inner circles used the concept of symbolism to really try and dig into the guts of the poem to find the real meaning. This poem by Stafford is dripping with symbolism, it is contained in every line, it's not the hard part finding what each line is saying it's hard trying to piece together what they mean as a whole.

Word Choice—Word choice is also very in-depth in this poem, every word seems to be well chosen to convey a certain hidden idea. As I discussed before the use of through is a good example of this, it is possible he could have said "Traveling *in* the Dark" and we wouldn't have even stopped for a second to think about it otherwise.

Vivid Imagery—Stafford's use of words also help at least me image what is happening in my head. This helped for me to better grasp what is trying to say. Although I never really was able to come to a final all-including conclusion in till Mr. Copeland discussed it with us I think the use of the words helped me better understand the text.

Reflection on Performance
I think my preparation was poor for the seminar, mostly due the fact I had a hard time understanding its true meaning, therefore I had a hard time really thinking of good content to add to the discussion. While I was in the inner circle I just kind of kept to myself, I had certain ideas of what maybe the poem was saying but when-ever I got around to saying it, it seemed somebody else had just made a revelation. My performance inside the circle was poor for the simple reason I didn't contribute much of anything to the discussion. While I was on the outer circle I was interested very much in where the group's discussion was going. They were so close and yet so far, and I was only disappointed at the very end. For my next seminar I can't promise to be able to contribute a lot but maybe an extra 5 minutes on the text or another reading of the text could help me piece it together better.

As for Group performance I think we did poorly, but not that I can be much of a critic. The frequent pauses from my view-point wasn't while we were thinking but simply nervousness about what should be said next. We had a rather large group and I think that combined with the general lack of understanding from most of our circle lead to poor coordination and discussion. While we were on the outside I think our critical points were valid although we were hardly any better. Nonetheless constructive criticism is always a good thing.

(continued on next page)

FIGURE 8.8 Example of Reflection

Reflection on Content

Thesis Statement:
William Stafford in his poem "Traveling Through the Dark" uses symbolism and word choice to convey the idea that all choices have an end and beginning and that we should make them carefully for they not only affect us directly but also others indirectly.

Some points I would include in my essay over William Stafford's meaning he is conveying are, how somebody's choice of driving to fast and therefore killing a deer, not only killed the deer but affected the fawn inside and possibly could have affected others driving. I would also make a point of the car and how it is waiting for Stafford to return to it so he may continue down "the road" or life, symbolizing the fact that choices must be made, no matter how painful before we may continue on life's journey. Another point that I could make is how the title of the poem suggests something about choices in life and how they all end and begin with *Through the Dark* not **in the Dark**. All choices and their consequences for bad or worse will come to an end, and regardless we will still be moving down life's road.

    Everybody makes bad decisions, I am no exception, nobody is. I have made bad mistakes in the past and will continue to do so, the only thing I can do is try and learn from them and prevent future ones from happening using past experience. Stafford in this poem is making the same point, however I believe he isn't denouncing the fact that mistakes are all okay, some mistakes are unavoidable but those that are extremely profound deserve dire consequences. I think this sort of ties into the whole thing with Bush and Iraq, it seems whenever they say something and it is proven the other way around or they are proven to have made a mistake they simply blow it off saying "everybody makes mistakes." That may be true but mistakes are never any good unless you learn from them, and so far Bush never has been forced to do that in his sheltered rich life and now as leading his Administration. A mistake of disregarding intelligence causing 3,000 deaths or invading a country on shady intelligence that is later proven false deserves dire consequences, your mistake left them with nothing but blood on their hands. Anyways, before I get too side-tracked or possibly offend you I'll conclude this again, Mistakes are good but we learn from them much less than we could.

FIGURE 8.8 Example of Reflection *(continued)*

CONCLUSION

The synthesis and evaluation of the content and skills explored in a Socratic circle are decisive in the improvement of student dialogue in the classroom. Helping students assess their performances both formally and informally and to apply the lessons learned from such assessments to future Socratic circles is one of the teacher's central roles in the strategy's process. As students improve their dialogue skills within the classroom through Socratic circles, their skills outside the classroom will improve as well.

    Socratic circles offer a laboratory-like environment in which students learn the process and skills necessary to live and fully participate in a democratic society. Beyond the exploration of curricular content and the expansion of learning skills, the embracing of a diversity of opinions and perspectives, the broadening of critical thinking, the practice of team-building and community-building strategies, and the tolerance of intricacy and uncertainty are all valid reasons for incorporating Socratic circles into our classrooms. But perhaps most important of all is that through Socratic circles and classroom dialogue, students find value and merit in their own voices and ideas; they learn that they are equal collaborators in the creation of knowledge and meaning. Quite simply, students learn that they, too, matter.

Appendix

SOCRATIC CIRCLE TEXT SUGGESTIONS

Texts Helpful for Teaching the Socratic Circle Process

The Pledge of Allegiance
The Gettysburg Address (speech), Abraham Lincoln
"The Road Not Taken" (poem), Robert Frost
"Stopping by Woods on a Snowy Evening" (poem),
    Robert Frost
Opening two paragraphs of *Their Eyes Were Watching God* (novel), Zora Neale Hurston
"Imagine" (song lyrics), John Lennon
"Born in the U.S.A." (song lyrics), Bruce Springsteen
Last Painter on Earth (painting), James Doolin

Texts Helpful for Classes Experienced with Socratic Circles

"Evolution" (poem), Sherman Alexie
"First Snow at Alsace" (poem), Richard Wilbur
"Let America Be America Again" (poem), Langston
    Hughes
Last four paragraphs of *The Great Gatsby* (novel),
    F. Scott Fitzgerald

"About Revenge" (essay), Sir Francis Bacon
"Tangled Up in Blue" (song lyrics), Bob Dylan
"Hotel California" (song lyrics), The Eagles
"Fortunate Son" (song lyrics), Creedence Clearwater Revival

Texts Helpful for Connections to Romeo and Juliet

"Teenager" (song lyrics), Better Than Ezra
"One Last Breath" (song lyrics), Creed
"My Sacrifice" (song lyrics), Creed
"I'd Lie for You (and That's the Truth)" (song lyrics), Meat Loaf
"Satellite" (song lyrics), Dave Matthews Band

Texts Helpful for Connections to The Odyssey

"Ulysses" (poem), Alfred, Lord Tennyson
"Carry on Wayward Son" (song lyrics), Kansas
"Fortunate Son" (song lyrics), Creedence Clearwater Revival
"Tales of Brave Ulysses" (song lyrics), Cream
"Nothing Gold Can Stay" (poem), Robert Frost

Texts Helpful for Connections to To Kill a Mockingbird

"Losing My Religion" (song lyrics), R.E.M.
"Man in Black" (song lyrics), Johnny Cash
"Imagine" (song lyrics), John Lennon
Boomtown (painting), Thomas Hart Benton

Texts Helpful for Connections to Of Mice and Men

"Hay for the Horses" (poem), Gary Snyder
"I Hear America Singing" (poem), Langston Hughes
"Nothing Gold Can Stay" (poem), Robert Frost
"One Friend" (song lyrics), Dan Seals

Texts Helpful for Connections to A Separate Peace

"First Snow at Alsace" (poem), Richard Wilbur
"Birches" (poem), Robert Frost
"Boats Against the Current" (song lyrics), Blake Chen
"Self Deception" (song lyrics), Lacuna Coil
"My Own Prison" (song lyrics), Creed

Texts Helpful for Connections to Julius Caesar

"The Fall of Rome" (poem), W. H. Auden
"Faith in Me" (song lyrics), Crosby, Stills, Nash and Young
"Authority Song" (song lyrics), John Mellencamp
Aloha (sculpture), John Buck

Texts Helpful for Connections to The Crucible

"What Is Truth" (song lyrics), Johnny Cash
"About Revenge" (essay), Sir Francis Bacon
"I'd Lie for You (and That's the Truth)" (song lyrics), Meat Loaf
"The Army of Truth" (poem), Henrik Wergeland

Texts Helpful for Connections to Their Eyes Were Watching God

"And Still I Rise" (poem), Maya Angelou
"Uptown Girl" (song lyrics), Billy Joel
Do the Right Thing (movie), Spike Lee
"Entitlement" (poem), Joe Okonkwo
"Like a Hurricane" (song lyrics), Neil Young

Texts Helpful for Connections to The Adventures of Huckleberry Finn

"The Concrete River" (poem), Luis J. Rodriguez
"Song for America" (song lyrics), Kansas
"Southern Accent" (song lyrics), Tom Petty
"Born to Run" (song lyrics), Bruce Springsteen

Texts Helpful for Connections to The Great Gatsby

"To an Athlete Dying Young" (poem), A. E. Housman
"The Idea of Order at Key West" (poem), Wallace Stevens
"Boats Against the Current" (song lyrics), Eric Carmen
"Superman (It's Not Easy)" (song lyrics), Five for Fighting
Reflections from a Dream (painting), K. C. Maxwell

Texts Helpful for Connections to Native Son

"Hurricane" (song lyrics), Bob Dylan
"Mother to Son" (poem), Langston Hughes

"Traveling Through the Dark" (poem), William Stafford
"Folsom Prison Blues" (song lyrics), Johnny Cash
"One" (song lyrics), Creed

FORMS

Socratic Circle Feedback Form

Name_____ Hour_____ Date_____

1. Rate the inner circle's performance on the following criteria: (circle the appropriate number)

Did the participants ...	Poor		Average		Excellent
dig below the surface meaning?	1	2	3	4	5
speak loudly and clearly?	1	2	3	4	5
cite reasons and evidence for their statements?	1	2	3	4	5
use the text to find support?	1	2	3	4	5
listen to others respectfully?	1	2	3	4	5
stick with the subject?	1	2	3	4	5
talk to each other, not just the leader?	1	2	3	4	5
paraphrase accurately?	1	2	3	4	5
avoid inappropriate language?	1	2	3	4	5
ask for help to clear up confusion?	1	2	3	4	5
support each other?	1	2	3	4	5
avoid hostile exchanges?	1	2	3	4	5
question others in a civil manner?	1	2	3	4	5
seem prepared?	1	2	3	4	5
make sure questions were understood?	1	2	3	4	5

2. Name specific people who did one or more of the above criteria well.

3. What was the most interesting question asked?

4. What was the most interesting idea to come from a participant?

5. What was the best thing you observed?

6. What was the most troubling thing you observed?

7. How could this troubling thing be corrected or improved?

Socratic Circles: Fostering Critical and Creative Thinking in Middle and High School by Matt Copeland. Copyright © 2005. Stenhouse Publishers.

Student: _____   Hour: _____   Date: _____   Topic: _____

Socratic Circle Rubric	Reading of text and preparation for circle.	Engaged in discussion and stays on-task.	Supports ideas with references to the text.	Encourages thinking and participation in others.	Listens respectfully and builds from ideas of others.	Presents self and ideas in a civil and proper manner.	Questions insightfully and uses sound reasoning.	Accepts more than one point of view on the text.
5 Outstanding	Remarks and written work reveal a close, critical reading of the text and thorough preparation.	Demonstrates active and eager participation throughout entire circle. Keeps group on-task.	Makes specific references to text to support and defend ideas on a consistent basis.	Guides the direction and success of the circle and takes steps to involve all participants.	Listens unusually well. Comments indicate very accurate and perceptive listening.	Demonstrates respect and enthusiasm. Works to support all participants at all times.	Questions and ideas are apt, insightful, and logical; and contribute to construction of meaning.	Accepts points of view other than own and uses them to expand ideas and discover new meaning.
4 Good	Remarks and written work reveal a close, critical reading of the text, but preparation appears incomplete.	Active and eager participation in more than 80% of circle. Keeps self on-task always and others at times.	Makes specific references to text to support and defend ideas often and when challenged.	Attempts to guide circle and draw in participants and is most often successful.	Listens well. Pays attention and generally responds well to ideas and questions from others.	Demonstrates respect and enthusiasm. Supports all participants most of the time.	Questions and ideas are apt, insightful, and logical but may not fully help meaning construction.	Accepts points of view other than own and attempts to use them to discover new meaning.
3 Average	Remarks and written work reveal a close reading of the text, but ideas seem to be less than complete.	Active and eager participation in more than 50% of circle. Stays on-task most of the time.	Makes specific references to text to support and defend ideas only when challenged.	Attempts to guide circle and draw in participants but is not always effective.	Generally listens well but is not always attentive as evident in responses or body language.	Demonstrates respect but may be less than totally supportive of others at times.	Questions and comments are apt and logical but lack insight to move group forward.	Acknowledges other points of view but struggles to use them to expand meaning.
2 Below Average	Remarks and written work do not reveal a close, critical reading of the text.	Some active participation in circle; may be less than eager. Off-task frequently.	Makes few references to text to support and defend ideas even when challenged.	Attempts to guide circle and draw in reluctant participants are not successful.	Comments tend to reflect an earlier failure to listen carefully to what was said.	Speech and manner suggest lack of understanding of purpose. Lacks sense of teamwork.	Questions and ideas reveal personal reactions, but not logical, apt arguments.	Argues with other points of view and reluctantly acknowledges them as a possibility.
1 Not Acceptable	Remarks and written work suggest the text was not read.	No active participation in circle. Others may be distracted by behavior.	Makes no specific references to text to support and defend ideas.	Makes no attempts to guide circle or draw in reluctant participants.	Does not listen adequately. Comments or body language suggestive of inattentiveness.	Does not display respect or enthusiasm for circle or other participants.	Remarks are illogical, difficult to follow, and offer the group no benefit.	Does not acknowledge or accept other points of view.

Socratic Circle Scorecard

5 = Outstanding 4 = Good 3 = Average 2 = Below Average 1 = Not Acceptable

Class: _____ Hour: _____ Date: _____ Topic: _____

Student's Name (Initials)	Reading of text and preparation for circle.	Engaged in discussion and stays on-task.	Supports ideas with references to the text.	Encourages thinking and participation in others.	Listens respectfully and builds from ideas of others.	Presents self and ideas in a civil and proper manner.	Questions insightfully and uses sound reasoning.	Accepts more than one point of view on the text.
1.								
2.								
3.								
4.								
5.								
6.								
7.								
8.								
9.								
10.								
11.								
12.								
13.								
14.								
15.								

First Inner Circle   Second Inner Circle   Time in Discussion: _____ minutes

Socratic Circle Reflection

Instructions

After each of our Socratic circles you will be responsible for turning in a two-page, single-spaced reflection on the experience. This reflection will comprise four sections: (1) vocabulary, (2) strategies/techniques for comprehension and analysis, (3) reflection on performance, and (4) reflection on content. The information below will help you understand what content needs to be placed in each of the four sections.

It is imperative that you keep these reflections in a safe place once they have been graded and returned. At the end of the semester they will be compiled into a portfolio and used as evidence to document your growth through Socratic circles. This portfolio will affect your final grade in this class. Not having each of the reflections on our circles will result in a lower grade. DO NOT LOSE THESE REFLECTIONS!!!

Also, because your final Socratic circle portfolio will ask you to show growth over time, it is in your best interest to make sure that you date each and every one of your Socratic circle reflections and identify the title of the text that served as the basis of discussion.

Vocabulary

In this section you will list *at least three words* from the selection of text that you either were unfamiliar with when you first read the piece or words that you felt your understanding of changed over the course of the Socratic circle itself. For each of the identified words you will need to list three additional pieces of information: (1) the part of speech for the word as it is used in the text, (2) a dictionary definition for the word as it is used in the context of the sentence, (3) two to three sentences describing how your understanding of the word developed and/or changed through the Socratic circle process.

> *example:*
> indivisible (adj)—incapable of undergoing division
> The dictionary provided me with a basic understanding of this word, but it wasn't until we started discussing the text and the history of the Pledge of Allegiance that I truly began to understand the importance of this idea. After our discussion I realize that indivisibility is one goal of our country the Pledge tries to instill.

Strategies/Techniques for Comprehension and Analysis

In the section you will list *at least three strategies or techniques* that were used by either inner circle to comprehend and analyze the selection of text. *Strive to identify new strategies that were used for the first time.* For each identified strategy/technique listed, you will need to write a *2–3-sentence description* of how it was used.

> *example:*
> Use of metaphor—We discussed the scene the author described and how that was relevant to the meaning of the overall passage. Having the metaphor at the beginning of the piece helped the reader imagine the scene in his or her own mind and made understanding the author's main points much easier.

There are no right or wrong answers in this section, simply your opinions. This list of possible strategies/techniques could go on forever. However, this may be a type of thinking with which you are unfamiliar. In order to help you get started, here's a list of some other possible strategies:

Word choice	Use of repetition	Use of capitalization
Voice	Use of verb tense	Organization/Structure
Sentence structure	Use of punctuation	Author's attitude
Paraphrasing	Summarizing	

(continued on next page)

Reflection on Performance

This section will be divided into two paragraphs: (1) a description of how you performed as an individual in the Socratic circle and (2) a description of how your group performed in both the role of the inner circle and the role of the outer circle. Again, there are no right or wrong answers here, only well-expressed opinions. You *might* consider the following questions for each paragraph:

Individual Performance
- How would you rate your preparation for this Socratic circle? Why?
- How would you rate your contributions (both the number of times you spoke and the quality of what you said) to the conversation of the inner circle? Why?
- How would you rate the level of teamwork you displayed in the inner circle? Why?
- How would you rate the quality of feedback you gave while you were in the outer circle? Why?
- How could you personally have improved what transpired during the Socratic circle?
- What goals do you have for your next Socratic circle performance?

Group Performance
- How would you rate your group's preparation for this Socratic circle? Why?
- How would you rate the quality of the overall conversation of your inner circle? Why?
- How would you rate the level of teamwork displayed by your inner circle? Why?
- How would you rate the quality of feedback your group gave while in the outer circle? Why?

Reflection on Content

This final section will comprise three items: (1) a thesis statement for an "imaginary" essay you might write about the meaning and importance of the ideas expressed in the selection of text, (2) a paragraph in which you describe (in general terms) the main points you might make in that "imaginary" essay, and (3) a paragraph in which you make connections between the content of this selection of text and some element of your own experience. Elements you might consider connecting this text to include: what we are currently learning in this class, learning that has occurred in other classes, personal experiences from your life outside of school, experiences of friends and family members with which you are familiar, current events, movies, literature, music, art, etc. Like the previous three sections, this last paragraph has no right or wrong answers, only opinions.

Checklist

Before turning in a reflection, use the following checklist to ensure you have included all of the necessary requirements to receive full credit:

_____   Your name, the date of the Socratic circle, and the title of the selection of text

_____   Three vocabulary words, their parts of speech, appropriate definitions, and explanation

_____   Three techniques for comprehension and analysis with explanation

_____   One paragraph reflecting on your individual performance

_____   One paragraph reflecting on the performance of your group

_____   A thesis statement for an "imaginary" essay on this text

_____   One paragraph explaining the main points of that "imaginary" essay

_____   One paragraph explaining the connections you made between the text and your own life

Socratic Circles: Fostering Critical and Creative Thinking in Middle and High School by Matt Copeland. Copyright © 2005. Stenhouse Publishers.

Further Reading

Adler, M. J. 1942. "How to Mark a Book." In R. S. Loomis and D. L. Clark, eds., *Modern English Readings*. New York: Farrar & Rinehart.

——. 1982. *The Paideia Proposal: An Educational Manifesto*. New York: Collier.

——. 1983. *How to Speak, How to Listen*. New York: Macmillan.

——. 1984. *The Paideia Program: An Educational Syllabus*. New York: Macmillan.

Adler, M. J., and C. Van Doren. 1972. *How to Read a Book*. New York: Simon & Schuster.

Arnold, G. H., A. Hart, and K. Campbell. 1988. "Introducing the Wednesday Revolution." *Education Leadership* 45, 7: 48.

Bridges, D. 1988. *Education, Democracy, and Discussion*. Lanham, MD: University Press of America.

Brookfield, S. D., and S. Preskill. 1999. *Discussion as a Way of Teaching: Tools and Techniques for Democratic Classrooms*. San Francisco: Jossey-Bass.

Burbules, N. 1993. *Dialogue in Teaching: Theory and Practice*. New York: Teachers College Press.

Copeland, M., and M. Grout. 2001. *At the Crossroads: Learning to Reflect and Reflecting to Learn*. Ottawa, KS: The Writing Conference.

Daniels, H. 2002. *Literature Circles: Voice and Choice in Book Clubs and Reading Groups.* 2d ed. Portland, ME: Stenhouse.

Dillon, J. 1994. *Using Discussion in Classrooms.* Buckingham, England: Open University Press.

Downing, J. P. 1997. *Creative Teaching.* Englelwood, CO: Teacher Ideas Press.

Elder, L., and R. Paul. 1998. "The Role of Socratic Questioning in Thinking, Teaching and Learning." *Clearing House* 71, 5: 297–302.

Freire, P. 1993. *Pedagogy of the Oppressed.* New York: Continuum.

Giroux, H. 1987. "Citizenship, Public Philosophy, and the Struggle for Democracy." *Educational Theory* 37: 103–120.

Gray, D. 1989. "Putting Minds to Work: How to Use the Seminar Approach in the Classroom." *American Educator* 13, 3: 16–23.

———. 1992, March. *The Why and How of Seminars.* Paper presented at Socratic Seminars Training Session, Northern Arizona University, Flagstaff, AZ.

Holden, J., and J. S. Schmit. 2002. *Inquiry and the Literary Text.* Urbana, IL: National Council of Teachers of English.

Isaacs, W. B. 1999. *Dialogue and the Art of Thinking Together.* New York: Doubleday.

Lambright, L. L. 1995. "Creating Dialogue: Socratic Seminars and Educational Reform." *Community College Journal* 65, 4: 30–34.

Lipman, M. 1991. *Thinking in Education.* Cambridge: Cambridge University Press.

Metzger, M. 1998. "Teaching Reading." *Phi Delta Kappan* 80, 3: 240–248.

Moeller, V. J., and M. V. Moeller. 2002. *Socratic Seminars and Literature Circles for Middle and High School English.* Larchmont, NY: Eye on Education.

Overholser, J. C. 1992. "Socrates in the Classroom." *Social Studies* 83, 2: 77–83.

Paris, S. G., and L. R. Ayeres. 1994. *Becoming Reflective Teachers and Students with Portfolios and Authentic Assessment.* New York: American Psychological Association.

Phillips, C. 2001. *Socrates Café.* New York: W. W. Norton.

Polite, V. C., and A. H. Adams. 1997. "Critical Thinking and Values Clarification Through Socratic Seminars." *Urban Education* 32, 2: 256–279.

Probst, R. E. 1988. "Dialogue with a Text." *English Journal* 77, 1: 32–38.

Seeskin, K. 1987. *Dialogue and Discovery: A Study in Socratic Method.* New York: SUNY Press.

Strong, M. 1996. *The Habit of Thought: From Socratic Seminars to Socratic Practice.* Chapel Hill, NC: New View.

Tredway, L. 1995. "Socratic Seminars: Engaging Students in Intellectual Discourse." *Educational Leadership* 53, 1: 26–29.

———. 1996. "Art as 'Text' in the Classroom." *Momentum* 27, 3: 16–19.

Yankelovich, D. 2001. *The Magic of Dialogue: Transforming Conflict into Cooperation.* New York: Simon & Schuster.

Zeiderman, H. 1998. *A Guide for Leading Discussions Using Touchstones,* Volume 1. Annapolis, MD: C.Z.M. Press.

References

Adler, M. J. 1982. *The Paideia Proposal: An Educational Manifesto.* New York: Collier.

———. 1983. *How to Speak, How to Listen.* New York: Macmillan.

———. 1984. *The Paideia Program: An Educational Syllabus.* New York: Macmillan.

Arnold, G. H., A. Hart, and K. Campbell. 1988. "Introducing the Wednesday Revolution." *Education Leadership* 45, 7: 48.

Barry, A. L. 1997. "Visual Art Enhances the Learning of Shakespeare." *Education* 117, 4: 632–640.

Berthoff, A. E. 1987. "Dialectical Notebooks and the Audit of Meaning." In Toby Fulwiler, ed., *The Journal Book.* Portsmouth, NH: Boynton/Cook.

Bomer, R. 1995. *Time for Meaning: Crafting Literate Lives in Middle and High School.* Portsmouth, NH: Heinemann.

Brookfield, S. D., and S. Preskill. 1999. *Discussion as a Way of Teaching: Tools and Techniques for Democratic Classrooms.* San Francisco: Jossey-Bass.

Buck, J. 1978. *Aloha* [sculpture], 91.149. Permission to publish image received from artist.

Cameron, J. 1999. *The Right to Write.* New York: Putnam.

Cash, J. 1999. "Folsom Prison Blues." *16 Greatest Hits.* Sony Records.

Claggett, F., L. Reid, and R. Vinz. 1998. *Daybook of Critical Reading and Writing.* Wilmington, MA: Great Source.

Comparison of dialogue and debate. September 2002. *Social Studies 30: Canadian Studies.* Retrieved July 2, 2004, from the World Wide Web: http://www.sasked.gov.sk.ca/docs/social/law30/unit02/02_05_sh.html.

Copeland, M., and M. Grout. 2004. "Critical Reflection in the Innovative Classroom." *Kansas English* 89, 1: 39–43.

Dave Matthews Band. 1994. "Ants Marching." *Under the Table and Dreaming.* RCA Records.

Elder, L., and R. Paul. 1998. "The Role of Socratic Questioning in Thinking, Teaching and Learning." *Clearing House* 71, 5: 297–302.

Freire, P. 1993. *Pedagogy of the Oppressed.* New York: Continuum.

Fry, E. B., J. E. Kress, and D. L. Fountoukidis. 2000. *The Reading Teacher's Book of Lists.* San Francisco: Jossey-Bass.

Gray, D. 1989. "Putting Minds to Work: How to Use the Seminar Approach in the Classroom." *American Educator* 13, 3: 16–23.

———. 1992, March. *The Why and How of Seminars.* Paper presented at Socratic Seminars Training Session, Northern Arizona University, Flagstaff, AZ.

Green, J. 2002. *Green Book of Songs by Subject: The Thematic Guide to Popular Music.* Nashville, TN: Professional Desk References.

A Guide for Leaders of Great Books Discussion Groups. 1960. Chicago: Great Books Foundation.

Hirsch, E. D. 1993. *Cultural Literacy: What Every American Needs to Know.* New York: Random House.

Housman, A. E. 1998. *To an Athlete Dying Young: A Shropshire Lad.* Boston: Branden Books.

Hughes, L. 1995. "Let America Be America Again." *The Collected Poems of Langston Hughes.* New York: Vintage.

Hurston, Z. N. 2000. *Their Eyes Were Watching God.* New York: McGraw-Hill Higher Education.

Kingsolver, B. 1998. "Beating Time." *Another America.* Seattle: Seal Press.

Lambright, L. L. 1995. "Creating Dialogue: Socratic Seminars and Educational Reform." *Community College Journal* 65, 4: 30–34.

Metzger, M. 1998. "Teaching Reading." *Phi Delta Kappan* 80, 3: 240–248.

Perkins-Gough, D. 2003. "Creating a Timely Curriculum." *Educational Leadership* 61, 4: 12–18.

Polite, V. C., and A. H. Adams. 1997. "Critical Thinking and Values Clarification Through Socratic Seminars." *Urban Education* 32, 2: 256–279.

Porter-O'Donnell, C. 2004. "Beyond the Yellow Highlighter: Teaching Annotation Skills to Improve Reading Comprehension." *English Journal* 93, 5: 82–89.

Scriven, E. *Julius Caesar, Act IV Scene III, after Richard Westall, 1802* (Boydell Shakespeare Galley) [painting], 00.1751 Spencer Museum of Art, The University of Kansas, William Bridges Thayer Memorial.

Stafford, W. 1999. "Traveling Through the Dark." *The Way It Is: New and Selected Poems.* St. Paul, MN: Graywolf.

Strong, M. 1996. *The Habit of Thought: From Socratic Seminars to Socratic Practice.* Chapel Hill, NC: New View.

Tredway, L. 1995. "Socratic Seminars: Engaging Students in Intellectual Discourse." *Educational Leadership* 53, 1: 26–29.

———. 1996. "Art as 'Text' in the Classroom." *Momentum* 27, 3: 16–19.